Jesse S. (Jesse Samuel) Gilbert

The Mystery of Iniquity; or, Romanism not Christianity

Jesse S. (Jesse Samuel) Gilbert

The Mystery of Iniquity; or, Romanism not Christianity

ISBN/EAN: 9783337033460

Printed in Europe, USA, Canada, Australia, Japan

Cover: Foto ©ninafisch / pixelio.de

More available books at **www.hansebooks.com**

THE
MYSTERY OF INIQUITY;

OR,

ROMANISM NOT CHRISTIANITY.

BY

REV. JESSE S. GILBERT, A. M.,

Of the Newark M. E. Conference.

NEWARK, N. J.:
WARD & TICHENOR, PRINTERS AND PUBLISHERS.
1872.

Entered according to Act of Congress in the year 1871,
By WARD & TICHENOR,
In the office of the Librarian of Congress, at Washington, D. C.

CONTENTS.

	PAGE
PREFACE,	5

CHAPTER I.
The Issue Stated, ... 9

CHAPTER II.
A Glance at the Past, . . . 18

CHAPTER III.
Shall the Bible be our Guide? . . 31

CHAPTER IV.
How has Rome Treated the Bible? . . 43

CHAPTER V.
The Test Applied, ... 56

CHAPTER VI.
The Great Usurper, ... 75

CHAPTER VII.
The Mass, ... 95

CHAPTER VIII.
Confession, . . . 103

CHAPTER IX.
Purgatory, ... 115

CHAPTER X.
To Whom shall we Pray? . 128

CHAPTER XI.
Celibacy, . . 147

CHAPTER XII.
The Convent System, ... 158

CHAPTER XIII.
Minor Follies, ... 171

CHAPTER XIV.
Drunk with Blood. . 193

CHAPTER XV.
Rome in Prophecy, ... 205

CHAPTER XVI.
The Peril of the Hour, ... 227

PREFACE.

THE author of the present treatise is well aware that much has already been written and printed on the subject of Romanism. Ever since the memorable day when Luther nailed his celebrated theses to the door of the Wittenberg Cathedral, busy pens have been at work exposing the folly of Papal doctrine and Papal practice. Much that has been written has, however, gone out of print and become obsolete, because it no longer bears on the existing state of the controversy. The *spirit* of Rome has never been changed, but her mode of operation, in this country at least, has been greatly modified within the past ten years. Waning in the old world, the idea has been conceived that the Papal throne may some day be erected on the ruins of the American Republic. To carry out this bold plan no expense will be deemed too great, and no toil too severe. Our public school system must be destroyed, our rights of person and property invested, our halls of legislation and courts of justice brought under the control of Romish influence, one citadel of our liberties after another taken and destroyed, until we are brought under the complete dominion of Rome, and are changed from a nation of intelligent free men to a nation of blind and helpless Papal slaves.

This new aspect of things renders it necessary that we have the advantage of fresh and additional light. It must be shown that the spirit of Rome is still the same, that she is ever the enemy of civil and religious liberty, and that, under a smiling exterior and fair promises, she conceals dark and deep designs. Much that has been written on the subject of Romanism within the past twenty-five years is either too learned and elaborate for general circulation, or else too abusive and sensational to gain general credence. The author humbly hopes that he has met a real want of the times. The present work is not designed to be an exhaustive treatment of the subject, but simply to furnish a brief manual of the past history and present status of the Romanistic controversy. Great pains have been taken to secure absolute accuracy of statement, and to do justice in every case to those who maintain opposite views. How well the proposed object has been accomplished must be left to the reader to determine.

Trusting that some good may be wrought by the work now offered to the public, praying for the divine blessing on those still kept in the darkness of Romanism, and looking earnestly forward to the time when the man of sin shall be destroyed and Jesus reign supreme over the nations of the earth, the author commits this, the result of much toil and study, to the thinking men and women of the land.

VERONA, N. J.   J. S. G.

CHAPTER I.

THE ISSUE STATED.

" We do not look on the Popish sect as a religion, but rather as a hierarchical tyranny under a cloak of religion, clothed with the spoils of the civil power, which it has usurped to itself, contrary to our Saviour's own doctrine."—MILTON.

THERE are elements of devotion in the character of man, so deep-seated and universal, that some form of religion is rendered imperative. A sort of intuitive belief in the existence of a Supreme Being and a future state, impels all men to acts of adoration. Travelers have met with tribes and races, existing in a fearful state of physical and moral degradation: but none have been found without some form of religious belief and some form of worship. The belief is often vague and absurd, the form of worship low and revolting: but still the fact remains, that men are everywhere instinctively impelled to acts of devotion. The stars of heaven, the beasts of the earth, and the fruits of the field, have all been the objects of human adoration. "In Judah was God known: his name was great in Israel:" but the Persian, ignorant of the true God, bowed before the setting sun, while the Egyptians gravely adored cats and cows, and the streets of Athens were filled with "carved divinities."

In addition to this general belief in the existence of a Supreme Being and a future state, there is an almost universal conviction of sin, leading men to offer sacrifice and to look in some way for salvation. Hence in all ages, animal sacrifice has been common among the heathen, and for four thousand years was offered by a portion of the human family by Divine direction. If then, we are a fallen, sinful race, how important that we seek the Divine favor in the divinely appointed way? A mistake here may be fatal. Who dare assert that in religion. it matters not what a man believes. so long as he is sincere?

It is not so in other matters. If we take poison, deeming it to be food, our sincerity and ignorance will not save us from the natural consequences of our folly. In a hundred matters, "there is a way which seemeth right unto a man, but the end thereof are the ways of death." The question of what is right and wrong in religious belief, becomes important and pressing, as the interests and value of the soul rise superior to the interests and value of the body. If all men were agreed as to the right method of regaining the Divine favor and image, it would nevertheless be our duty seriously to ponder whether mankind had found the path of truth: but when we remember that the world is divided in these things, that men profess opposite and exclusive creeds, how important and solemn becomes the question, "What is truth?" The population of the world at the present time may be estimated at 1,250,000,000, and the religious condition of the world may be represented in round numbers as follows: Idolaters, 737,500,000; Christians, 328,980,000; Mohammedans, 177,500,000; Jews, 6,020,000; Mormons, 200,000.

By "Christians," we mean those who profess to derive their doctrines from, and to be followers of Christ. Those that have been classified under the general name of Christians do not, however, all agree either in practice or in doctrine. Under this term have been included (improperly, we hope to show,) those who follow the faith of Rome. These number about 170,000,000, regard the Pope as their sole head and infallible guide, while all others are denounced as vile heretics, and without reserve given over to endless damnation. The creed to which all bishops, ecclesiastics and teachers in the Romish Church, must give public assent, calls itself "This true catholic faith, out of which none can be saved." Within the past few years fearful anathemas have been fulminated from the Papal throne, against all who dare to do their own thinking.

One of the predecessors of the present Pope, in a celebrated bull, has said, "We declare and determine it a principle absolutely necessary to salvation that all human beings are subject to the Pope." If the high claims of this arrogant Church are true, all Protestants will surely be forever damned. Luther, Calvin, Wesley, Whitefield, Locke, Newton, Leighton, Howard are, beyond all question, in hell: while Newman Hall, Bishop Simpson, Dr. McCosh, and thousands of devoted men, who are seeking to serve God and to do good, must be on the way. Now, the Church of Rome, claiming for itself the name "Catholic," holding that beyond its pale there can be no possibility of salvation, looking upon all other religious bodies as "pestilent sects," that are to be denounced and destroyed, challenges the investigation of all thinking men. To investigate these claims is the object of the present treatise. If we find them sustained, we must lose no time in hiding ourselves under the protecting shadow of Rome; but if we find them absurb and false, no contempt will be too severe for the Church that has dared to put them forth. We shall endeavor to carry on our investigation, in a Christian and candid spirit. We propose to show that Romanism is in no sense Christianity, that it is a foreign hostile power, the unfailing foe of all true religion, whose rise, progress, persecutions, and final overthrow have all been portrayed in Holy Writ.

We propose to show that the doctrines and spirit of Romanism are in direct conflict with the doctrines and spirit of the Bible, that its history is dark and blood-stained, that it is the " Man of Sin" to be " destroyed," Babylon to be " thrown down," and the " Great Whore" to be "judged." We are well aware, that we shall not meet the views of that large class of persons, who look on Romanism as one form of Christianity among many others, or who, having given little or no attention to the subject, regard all denunciations of Popery as unchristian, because " there is good in all religions," and " good and bad in all churches." If these good-natured people could only get a peep " behind the scenes," and behold the internal workings and morals of Romanism, they would soon find some more worthy object on which to bestow their overflowing charity. There is another class that will take exception to the views set forth in this book. I mean that class of whom *Father* Morrell and Dr. Ewer constitute the fitting representatives. These men are professedly Protestant, yet harp on the " Failure of Protestantism," and as far as they dare, mimic the ways and forms of Romanism. Every now and then some of them muster up courage to identify themselves with the church that they have so long admired, and all lovers of outspoken truth rejoice that another, like Judas Iscariot, has gone " to his own place." While, however, we hold and maintain this view of the Roman Catholic Church, we would not imitate her bigotry and narrow-mindedness. Let it be remembered that in these high and exclusive claims, the Church of Rome stands alone, like Milton's Satan, " By sin exalted to so high pre-eminence." No other religious body claims to be the janitor of Heaven. The charity that *they* withhold from us, we extend to them, for while we cannot fail to perceive that the great mass of Romanists are living in sin and without Christ, we cannot forget that Fenelon, Pascal, and Masillon, were in communion with the Church of Rome. These were saints, not because they were Roman Catholics, but in spite of the fact. They were like those flowers that grow up from the bosom of a dead and decaying tree. The writer of this book has met with some members of the Romish Church, whom he had every reason to believe were sincere Christians. But all this proves nothing in favor of Romanism. A man may be saved while a member of the Church of Rome, in the same manner and for the same reason, that a heathen living up to the light of reason and conscience will be saved. "God is no respecter of persons: but in every nation, he that feareth Him and worketh righteousness, is accepted with Him."

We shall use the word "Church" when speaking of Popery, only by way of accommodation. We do not believe that it is a church, any more than Mormonism or Mohammedanism can be called a church. It is more of a political than it is an ecclesiastical body. But as it claims to constitute a church, and is usually called the Roman Catholic Church, we will sometimes use the word by way of convenience. We cannot, however, consent to use the word Catholic, unless accompanied by some qualifying term, for this would concede the entire argument. We believe in, and belong to the true Catholic or Universal church. This church is composed of all who love and serve the Lord Jesus in sincerity and truth, no matter by what name they are called, or in what part of the world they reside. The matter then is fairly before us. The Church of Rome claims to be the only true church, and consigns to eternal damnation all who refuse to bow at her altars. This claim we propose to investigate in the light of Scripture, reason and history, but with the spirit of Christian fairness and candor, without fear and without prejudice. May both reader and writer be guided into a knowledge of the truth.

CHAPTER II.

A GLANCE AT THE PAST.

"*Ask for the old paths.*"—JER. vi., 16.

NEARLY every one knows that the Church of Rome boasts of its antiquity, and in a triumphant tone, asks us, "Where the Protestant religion was before Luther?" To answer this question will be the object of the present chapter. Let it be remarked, however, that the argument drawn from antiquity does not carry much weight with it, after all. Judaism is older than Romanism, and Heathenism older than either. We will, however, examine the claims of antiquity set up by Romanism, and see how well they are sustained by Scripture and history. To be of any value, the antiquity of the Church of Rome must be equal to that of the New Testament, else it cannot be the Church of Christ and his Apostles.

That a society of Christians existed in the City of Rome, in the time of Paul, no one will deny. But did they set up the same claims, hold to the same doctrines and practices, that are now maintained by the Papacy. If they did not, if they maintained views and practices the very opposite, then the Church now having its central power at Rome, is not the same with the small band of believers gathered there in the time of Paul, any more than midnight is one with noonday. We know what the Church of Rome teaches at the present time—we find it in her catechisms, prayer-books, in the writings of her leading men, in the canons and decrees of the Council of Trent. Perhaps it would be best, just at this point, to present a brief summary of her teaching, that we may have it for reference in the future: She believes, in common with us, in God the Father, God the Son, and God the Holy Ghost; in the incarnation—death and resurrection of Jesus Christ, the final judgment, and a future state of reward and punishment. But on this foundation of truth, a vast superstructure of false doctrine and absurd practice has been erected. Here is a summary of Papal belief, as concocted by the Council of Trent, and issued in the form of a bull in December, 1564, (alas, for the boasted antiquity,) by Pope Pius IV. This is the creed before alluded to, to which all bishops, ecclesiastics and teachers in the Church of Rome must give public assent: "I most firmly admit and embrace apostolic and ecclesiastical traditions, and all other constitutions and observances of the same Church; I also admit the sacred Scriptures according to the sense which the holy mother Church has held and does hold, to whom it belongs to judge, of the true sense and interpretation of the Holy Scriptures; nor will I ever take or interpret them otherwise than according to the unanimous consent of the fathers. I profess, also, that there are truly and properly seven sacraments of the new law, instituted by Jesus Christ our Lord, and for the salvation of mankind, though all are not necessary for every one, namely: baptism, confirmation, eucharist, penance, extreme unction, orders, and matrimony, and that they confer grace; and of these, baptism, confirmation and order cannot be reiterated without sacrilege. I do also receive and admit the ceremonies of the Catholic Church, received and approved in the administration of all the above said sacraments. I receive and embrace all and every one of the things which have been defined and declared in the holy Council of Trent concerning sin and justification. I profess, likewise, that in the mass, is offered to God a true, proper and propitiatory sacrifice for the living and the dead; and that in the most holy sacrament of the eucharist, there is truly, really and substantially, the body and blood, together with the soul and divinity of our Lord Jesus Christ; and that there is made a conversion of the whole substance of the bread into the body, and of the whole substance of the wine into the blood, which conversion the Catholic Church calls transubstantiation. I confess, also, that under either kind alone, whole and entire, Christ and a true sacrament is received. I constantly hold that there is a purgatory, and that souls detained therein are helped by the suffrages of the faithful. Likewise that the saints reigning together with Christ are to be honored and invocated, that they offer prayers to God for us, and that their relics are to be venerated. I most firmly assert that the images of Christ, and of the mother of God ever virgin, and also of the other saints, are to be had and retained, and that due honor and veneration are to be given to them. I also affirm that the power of indulgences was left by Christ in the Church, and that the use of them is most wholesome to Christian people. I acknowledge the holy catholic and apostolic Roman Church, the mother and mistress of all churches; and I promise and swear true obedience to the Roman bishop, the successor of St. Peter, prince of the Apostles and vicar of Jesus Christ. I also profess and undoubtedly receive all other things delivered, defined, and declared by the sacred canons and general councils, and particularly by the holy Council of Trent; and likewise, I also condemn, reject and anathematize all things contrary thereto, and all heresies whatsoever condemned, rejected and anathematized by the Church. This true catholic faith, out of which none can be saved, which I now freely profess and truly hold, I, A B, promise, vow and swear, most constantly to hold and profess the same, whole and entire, with God's assistance, to the end of my life; and to procure, so far as lies in my power, that the same shall be held, taught, and preached by all who are under me, or are entrusted to my care, by virtue of my office, so help me God, and these holy gospels of God, Amen."

Now we know what are the teachings of Romanism, can we tell what was maintained by the primitive society of believers at Rome? If we do, we can soon settle the question of antiquity. Well, if we do not know what they taught, we know what was taught them.

There was quite a long letter written to them by the Apostle Paul, which has come down to our day. Paul is good authority, (even if Peter *was* the reigning Pope,) but when it is remembered, that both parties admit that this letter was inspired, and that it is a portion of Holy Scripture, its authority as umpire in the case becomes supreme. Well, let us look at it. Do we find anything in it about extreme unction, penance, indulgences, transubstantiation, the worship of Mary, the adoration of saints and images? Anything about purgatory, masses for the dead, the pre-eminence of the Roman Church, the supremacy of St. Peter, confession, or worship in an unknown tongue? Not a single word from beginning to end. The greatest heretic could have done no worse. Nay more, there are some things in this *inspired* letter that must have a curious sound to Roman Catholic ears. I wonder that they have never suspected Paul of being a Protestant. No doubt but that they would, had he lived and written a few centuries later, but in Paul's time, there was nothing in the Church at Rome, to protest against. He could say, "I thank my God through Jesus Christ for you all, that your faith is spoken of throughout the whole world." Should any one write such a letter at the present day to the people in Rome, he would very soon be condemned as a vile heretic. Surely times have changed. But let us look a little further into this epistle. It will amply repay examination. In the first verse of the 5th chapter, he says, "*Therefore being justified by faith, we have peace with God, through our Lord Jesus Christ.*" Why, Luther himself could not lay any more stress on faith. If we are justified by *faith*, what becomes of purgatory, penance and indulgences? In the 33d and 34th verses of the 8th chapter, he says again: "Who shall lay anything to the charge of God's elect? It is God that justifieth. Who is he that condemneth? It is Christ that died, yea, rather, that is risen again, who is ever at the right hand of God, who also maketh intercession for us." This looks as though we might go right up to the throne of God, without having to stop in purgatory, and there endure fire of purification. Christ is said to make "intercession for us," but what has become of Mary and all the saints? "Paul, thou art beside thyself."

In chapter 10th, verse 13th, he says: "For

whosoever shall call upon the name of the Lord shall be saved." This is too bad. What is to become of the poor priests, with their confession boxes, indulgences, and masses for the dead? The poor old Pope has just been hurling thunderbolts of wrath against all not in communion with the "Apostolic See," and here Paul tells us that if we "call on the name of the Lord" we "shall be saved." Other passages might be adduced, showing how little Paul knew of the dogmas and doings of Popery. Let such declarations as these be compared with the history and practices of Romanism. "Him that is weak in the faith, receive ye." "For the Kingdom of God is not meat and drink, but righteousness, and peace, and joy in the Holy Ghost." Beside the letter to the Romans, Paul wrote a number of others, as also did Peter and John. These letters both Roman Catholics and Protestants believe to be inspired, and place in the Canon of Scripture. But they all run like the Epistle to the Romans. Nothing about purgatory, mass, penance, relics, prayers to saints. Nothing is said of the Church at Rome as being superior in power or dignity to the Church at Corinth, Ephesus or Jerusalem. Peter lays no claim to any superiority over his brethren, calls himself an "elder," and permits Paul to withstand him to the face.

Now we are prepared to retort, and to ask Romanists where their religion was when Paul, Peter, James and John wrote their letters to the several churches. The Roman Catholic faith is old, we admit, but then it is not old enough. If we take a journey down the centuries, in order to get at the true faith, we will not stop short of Christ and his apostles. We are determined not to lose our way among the councils and fathers: but to pursue our inquiries until we reach the fountain head. Now, we are prepared to answer the question, "Where was the Protestant religion before Luther?" We reply, where it always was, still is, and ever will be: in the Bible. The Protestant religion is nothing new. It is simply the religion of the Bible, nothing more and nothing less. We ask the Romanists where their religion is, and what it is, and we are pointed to Papal bulls, to decrees of Councils, and to the sayings of the fathers. Ask us the same question, and we point to the Bible. From it we derive our doctrines and morals. History informs us how the Papal corruption was brought about. We can tell when the fiction of purgatory was invented, when that of the mass, and so on all through the chapter of shameful and shameless impositions. Not only can we point to the New Testament as the foundation of our faith and practice, but we have ample proof of an external kind, of the long continued, uninterrupted, and pure existence of our faith on earth. Dr. Breckinridge has well put this point: "The fact is, if the Roman Catholic Church had never existed in the world, we would have abundantly more proof of the pure succession of the Church of God on earth, than we have now. Because the chief objects of her existence have been to banish the Scriptures, to corrupt the church, to degrade the human race, to kill the saints of God, and to cover the earth with palpable darkness. How vast and how glorious would have been the living monuments to God, erected in whole nations which that church has butchered—that would now stand forth to bless our eyes, if she had never existed! Alas! our hearts sink within us when we contemplate the evil she has done, and dwell on the probable condition of the human race, at this moment, but for the dire influence of the Latin Church. Yet the very breadth of her errors and crimes affords us evidence of the continued existence of the truth, in the hearts and lives of those who resisted her sway, or died beneath her strokes. The African churches of the early ages, the various Asiatic churches, especially the Nestorians, the Greek church, the Caldees in Ireland, the Waldenses in the South of Europe, the Moravians and Bohemians in the east of Europe, the writings of the early Greek and Latin fathers, the army of martyrs, have handed down to us evidence of the constant existence of those who did not bow the knee to Baal."—*Papism in the United States, page* 32.

God has always had a people to serve Him.

Truth has never been quite banished from the earth. Of this succession we are proud. We care but little for that boasted chain over which Romanists and High-Churchmen make so great an ado, every link in which is covered with rust and blood : but we do glory in the succession of faithful witnesses for the truth. Many a long century has the true church abode in the wilderness, but she has never yet become extinct. She has lived all through the dark and stormy past, is advancing from one victory to another, and shall yet become the "joys of the whole earth." Popery has burned men and women and bibles, but the eternal truth of God, cannot be burned with fire, bound by chains, or drowned in flood.

> "No : marble and recording brass decay,
> And, like the graver's memory, pass away :
> The works of man inherit, as is just,
> Their author's frailty, and return to dust :
> But truth divine forever stands secure,
> Its head as guarded as its base is sure ;
> Fixed in the rolling flood of endless years,
> The pillar of the eternal truth appears,
> The raving storm and dashing wave defies,
> Built by that Architect who built the skies."

CHAPTER III.

SHALL THE BIBLE BE OUR GUIDE?

"*To the law and to the testimony.*"—ISAIAH viii. 20.
"*Thy word is a lamp unto my feet, and a light unto my path.*"—PSALM cxix. 105.

THE great question between Roman Catholics and Protestants is simply this: "Is the Bible sufficient as a rule of faith, and guide to salvation?" We say that it is. They say that it is not. Prove that the Bible alone is sufficient; that it is possible for us to read, study and understand the Bible, without the aid of popes, fathers or councils, and a complete victory is soon secured. No Roman Catholic has ever dared to defend the doctrines and rites of his church by a simple appeal to the pure word of God. Smarius in his "Points of Controversy," (a Roman Catholic work recently published) starts off with a chapter entitled, "The Bible not the only Rule of Faith and Practice." Lest some may think that our opponents are misrepresented, I will quote from a standard Roman Catholic work—Milner's "End of Controversy:"

"The Catholic rule of faith, as I stated before, is not merely *the written word of God,* but *the whole word of God, both written and unwritten;* in other words, *Scripture and tradition,* and these *expounded and explained by the Catholic Church.* This implies that we have a *two-fold rule,* or *law,* and that we have *an interpreter* or *judge to explain it,* and to decide upon it in all doubtful points."—*End of Controversy, page* 80.

The italics are those of the author quoted. There is a very short way by which to decide the question now fairly before us. The Bible is inspired. In other words, God is its author. Men wrote it; but God guided the pen and kept them from all error. This is admitted by both parties. Now what does the Bible say of itself? Does it claim to be man's only infallible and all sufficient guide? If it does, the matter is settled. In the 2d epistle to Timothy, 3d chapter and 15th verse, Paul says: "And that from a child thou hast known the Holy Scriptures which are able to make thee wise unto salvation." This has a plain, straight-forward look. The Holy Scriptures are able to make a child "wise unto salvation." Is not that wise enough? Can Bishop Bailey or even Archbishop McCloskey do any better with the help of tradition and " Holy Mother Church?" But hold on, we are too fast. According to Dr. Milner, we have no right to discuss the question at all. On the 103d page of his most remarkable book, he has the following astonishing passage:

"Before I enter on the discussion of any part of Scripture with you or your friends, I am bound, dear sir, in conformity with my rule of faith, as explained by the fathers, and particularly by Tertullion, to protest against your or their right to argue from Scripture, and, of course, to deny any need there is of my replying to any objection which you may draw from it. For I have reminded you that *no Scripture is of any private interpretation;* and I have proved to you that the whole business of the Scriptures belongs to the Church—she has preserved them, she vouches for them, and she alone, and by the help of tradition, authoritatively explains them. Hence, it is impossible that the real sense of Scripture should ever be against her and her doctrine; and hence, of course, I might quash every objection which you may draw from any passage in it by this short reply, *The Church understands the passage differently from you, therefore you mistake its meaning."*

Shades of Whately, defend us! Is not this a perfect gem of fair and conclusive reasoning? I wonder that he ever wrote anything on the subject, when the matter can be settled without the exercise of thought or argument. But he gives us the reason: "Nevertheless, as *charity beareth all things and never faileth*, I will, for the better satisfying of you and your friends, quit my vantage ground for the present, and answer distinctly to every text not yet answered by me, which any of you gentlemen, or which

Dr. Porteus himself, has brought against the Catholic method of religion."

The dogmatic manner in which Dr. Milner assumes the very matter in discussion, and then triumphantly talks about leaving his "vantage ground," leads us to imagine that if he had lived a few centuries ago, he would have employed weapons more to his liking than are logic and Scripture. Rome has often found that fire and sword are no mean allies; but of this, more anon.

We will return to our examination of Scripture; nor will we allow Dr. Milner to rule this divine witness out of court. And Scripture, too, shall speak for itself, untrammeled by the sayings of the fathers, or by the decrees of councils. A Christian church was founded by St. Paul in the city of Berea. We read that when the apostles preached to them, not satisfied even with *their* testimony, they "searched the Scriptures daily whether these things were so." Strange to relate, this conduct on their part was commended; and they were pronounced "more noble" than the unthinking inhabitants of Thessalonica. The preaching of the apostles might be investigated in the light of Scripture; but now we must receive with unquestioning faith the teaching of every little upstart of a priest, though he be too ignorant to read correctly a single line of the original Greek or Hebrew. St. Luke, in his preface to the book which bears his name, gives us the reason why he wrote:

"It seemed good to me also, having had perfect understanding of all things from the very first, to write unto thee in order, most excellent Theophilus, that thou mightest know the certainty of those things wherein thou hast been instructed." Ah! then tradition is not the most reliable thing in the world; and in order to "know the certainty" of divine things, we must have recourse to the written word.

I think that we have pursued this line of thought long enough. Scripture claims to be an infallible guide; and in no place allows to tradition a share in this high prerogative. Consider what tradition is. Peter and Paul before they die, instruct some of their pupils in matters not mentioned in

Scripture, or stated too obscurely to be understood. These, before they die, instruct others. These again, tell somebody else: and so the tradition is passed along through eighteen centuries of turmoil and conflict. And this is the "unwritten word," equal in importance and authority to the Holy Bible itself. Away with such absurd blasphemy. Tradition either merely accords with Scripture or else it must flatly contradict it. If it merely accords with Scripture, why is it of such high value? The same virtue may be claimed for thousands of worthy Christian teachers. If it contradicts Scripture, it must be of the Devil. But, says another, it informs us on those points upon which Scripture is silent. Then it must go beyond Scripture, and what shall we do with those solemn words of the beloved disciple: "If any man shall add unto these things, God shall add unto him the plagues that are written in this book." (Rev. xxii., 18.) But, says another, it does not contradict or go beyond Scripture; it simply explains Scripture. But is Scripture so obscure that we must take this difficult and roundabout way to get at its meaning? So Roman Catholics say. Indeed, one of their most eminent authors tells us that "The Scripture is not of itself, demonstratively clear in points of first rate importance; and the divine law, like human laws, without an authorized interpeter, must ever be a source of doubt and contention."

This simply amounts to saying that tradition is clearer than Scripture. Now if Paul, Peter, James and the other apostles could preach in a clear and intelligent manner, why in the name of common sense could they not write in a clear and intelligent manner? Men usually take more care in writing, than they do in speaking. More than this, they wrote by inspiration. I think, then, that we can get along very well without tradition. The Scriptures are able to make us "wise unto salvation."

One more point must be cleared up before we proceed with our discussion. Who shall interpret the Bible? The Church of Rome claims to be the sole interpreter of this sacred volume. She must do the world's thinking in this respect. This claim we refuse to recognize. We claim that every man has not only the right to read, but to interpret this Book. In this glorious employment, we may have the aid of God's Holy Spirit. "If any of you lack wisdom, let him ask of God, that giveth to all men liberally, and upbraideth not." (James i., 5.) Let us see how the rule of the Romish Church will work. A poor sinner reads in the New Testament such gracious invitations as these: "Come unto me, all ye that labor and are heavy-laden, and I will give you rest." "And the Spirit and the bride say come. And let him that heareth say come. And let him that is athirst come. And whosoever will, let him take the water of life freely." Now, before he can form any idea as to the meaning of this, he must find out how the Church understands it, how all the Popes, councils and fathers have interpreted it. Then if he finds in all church history, a single dissenting voice, he must forever remain in awful uncertainty: for there must be, according to the creed of the Council of Trent, the "unanimous consent of the holy fathers." Does not this shut us off from ever knowing the will of God? But, says the Roman Catholic, do you not know that "No prophecy of the Scripture is of any private interpretation"? This is a correct Scriptural quotation, we admit: but let us look at it. You will find it in 2d Peter i., 20. Let us take context and all. "We have also a more sure word of prophecy: whereunto ye do well that ye take heed, as unto a light that shineth in a dark place, until the day dawn, and the day star arise in your hearts: knowing this first, that no prophecy of the Scripture is of any private interpretation. For the prophecy came not in old time by the will of man; but holy men of God spake as they were moved by the Holy Ghost."

Notice three things: First, the remarks of the apostle only refer to the prophetic parts of Scripture. Second, we are urged to "take heed" to (that is, consider,) the subject of prophecy. Third, the reason assigned why it is not of private interpretation, is that it came not by the "will of man," but from those who were "moved by the Holy Ghost." Now it seems strange that because prophecy is inspired, we must therefore be unable to understand it. Now suppose the word rendered *interpretation*, be translated as Doddridge, McKnight, Nevins, and many other excellent Greek scholars have translated it, *invention* or *impulse:* how clear and intelligible becomes the entire passage. "Knowing this first, that no prophecy of the Scripture is of any private invention. For the prophecy came not in old time by the will of man: but holy men of God spake as they were moved by the Holy Ghost." One thing is certain, the apostle does not mean to deny the right of private judgment, or he would not exhort us to "take heed" to the "more sure word of prophecy." Romanists have no other passage of Scripture with which to support their strange views of biblical interpretation. Having but this one, they make a great ado over it, but we think that we have shown the utter fallacy of the conclusions they draw from it. In the present discussion, we shall cling to the Bible. This is the rule of our faith and practice:

> " Most wondrous book! bright candle of the Lord!
>   Star of eternity, the only star
>   By which the bark of man could navigate
>   The sea of life, and gain the coasts of bliss
>   Securely; only star which rose on time,
>   And, on its dark and troubled waters, still
>   As generation, drifting slowly by
>   Succeeded generation, threw a ray
>   Of heaven's own light, and to the hills of God,
>   The everlasting hills, pointed the sinner's eye."

CHAPTER IV.

HOW HAS ROME TREATED THE BIBLE?

"*For I testify unto every man that heareth the words of the prophecy of this book. If any man shall add unto these things, God shall add unto him the plagues that are written in this book; And if any man shall take away from the words of the book of this prophecy, God shall take away his part out of the book of life, and out of the holy city, and from the things which are written in this book.*"—REV. xxii., 18–19.

THE Bible is God's great gift of love and mercy to a lost and dying world. It was designed to exist for all time, and to be read by all men. It teaches us how to escape from sin, death and hell. It contains such a rich world of hidden treasure, that centuries of devout study have not revealed all its meaning; while, at the same time, the great plan of salvation is so clearly revealed, that the most simple need not go estray. Millions have feasted on its heavenly truth, and died with its precious words of promise on their tongues. It has brought comfort to the broken-hearted mourner, peace to the burdened conscience and troubled heart of the poor sinner. Well has one of Israel's sweet singers said:

> "Precious Bible! what a treasure
>   Does the word of God afford!
> All I want for life or pleasure,
>   Food and medicine, shield and sword;
> Let the world account me poor,
> Having this I need no more."

Guilty, false, and cruel must be the system, that will degrade in any way this sacred volume; strive in any way to shut it out from the hearts and homes of the people. We call, then, in the name of our sin-burdened and suffering humanity, the Church of Rome to answer for her treatment of this Divine Book. We charge the Romish Church with having degraded, corrupted and mistranslated the Bible. We charge her with the crime of making the Bible a sealed book, by claiming to be its only expositor. With the crime of retarding in every possible way, the circulation and reading of the

Bible. To sum up the whole in a single sentence, we charge the Romish Church with being *at all times, and in every possible way, the inveterate enemy of the Holy Bible.* Can this charge be sustained? We shall see. It has already been shown that the Roman Catholic Church exalts tradition to an equal footing with Scripture. This has been proved by witnesses taken from the Romish Church itself. It is a well-known fact, and one which no intelligent person, whether a Romanist or a Protestant, would ever think of denying. Is not this degrading Scripture? If we should make the doggerel of old Mother Goose a text book in our schools and colleges, would it not justly be considered as an insult to the writings of our philosophers and scientists?

It has also been shown from Roman Catholic authority that this Church claims to be the only reliable expositor of Scripture. Does not this in effect make it a sealed book? Let Dr. Milner answer. We are happy to refer the reader to this treatise, because the work of Milner is a sort of standard among Roman Catholics as the writings of Calvin are to the Presbyterians, or the writings of Wesley and Watson among Methodists. He says: "*The Church does not dictate an exposition of the whole Bible, because she has no tradition concerning a very great proportion of it.*"—End of Controversy, page 109.

Well, things have come to a pretty pass, indeed. We dare not, as we value our eternal interest, interpret a single passage of Scripture for ourselves. We must trust all to the infallible church. But this infallible church itself does not know anything about "*a very great proportion*" of the Bible. I have just been looking again at the work of Dr. Milner. I thought that I must have made a mistake, the announcement is so astonishing. But no, there it is in black and white, on the 109th page of his book. Any one may get and read it. "A very great proportion" of the Bible can never be understood. Why was it written? Let the infallible church reply. But why may we not understand it? Did not God intend that we should understand it? We are told that all Scripture is profitable: but what good can it do us, if it is impossible for us to understand it? Are we unable to secure the aid of the Divine Spirit: and is this the reason why we may not understand it? No, for God declares himself ever willing to bestow this priceless gift. What then *is* the reason? Alas, *we have no tradition.* Who is willing to receive such absurd and blasphemous teaching? Who is willing to follow a guide so blind and intolerant?

To the Roman Catholic the Bible must ever remain a sealed book. He dare not interpret the simplest passage, until he has secured the "unanimous consent of the holy fathers." Those who know much about the teachings of the holy fathers, must laugh at the idea of getting their "unanimous consent." But we charged the Church of Rome with having corrupted the Bible. Let us look at this for a short time. In many large family Bibles, between the Old and New Testaments, there are placed fourteen volumes called the Apocrypha. The word apocrypha is derived from the Greek *Apokrapha*, and means hidden, mysterious. There is no reason why these books should be bound together with the Old and New Testament. Any one can see that they form no part of Scripture. They do not claim to be inspired. They are not found in any catalogue of canonical writings made during the first four centuries after Christ. The Jewish Church never received them as a part of the Canon. Christ never quoted them, neither did any of the apostles. Those books contain statements at variance with history, self-contradictory, and opposed to the doctrines and precepts of Scripture. These books the Roman Catholic Church has exalted to a place in the sacred Canon. This was done by the Council of Trent in the 16th century. (*The next time a Romanist asks me where my religion was before Luther, I am going to ask him, where his faith was before the Council of Trent.*)

Is not this a gross corruption of Scripture? Why, the Bible is a very small part of the rule of faith and practice, adopted by the Church of Rome. By the time we get through with tradition, the fathers and the apocrypha, we need but devote very little attention to the Bible. I do not wonder that so little prominence is given to the Bible, in the preaching and writing of Roman Catholics. I do not wonder that so few Roman Catholics know so little about the Bible. Imagine a Romanist commencing to read the Bible through. He must pause at the first verse, and before he can attach any meaning to the words, get the "unanimous consent of the holy fathers." When would he complete his first reading of the Bible? I do not think I should care much to read the Bible myself, if I had to go through it in that style.

We have charged the Church of Rome with being the inveterate foe of the Bible: and history confirms the truth of the charge. Nay, more, we do not appeal to history alone. Let the present speak. The Romish Church claims to be the same in every age: and in some respects the boast is true. She certainly manifests in every age the same strange hostility to the word of God. To begin, then, *the Roman*

Catholic Church has never published a Bible. This may seem a sweeping and uncharitable charge, but it is nevertheless true. We understand by a Bible, the pure, unadulterated word of God, published in the language of the people, without note or comment. Commentaries are good enough in their place, but commentaries are not Bibles. Barnes' Notes, Clark's and Benson's Commentaries are not Bibles. If you went to purchase one of them, you would not ask for a Bible. Now, the Romish Church has published a version of the Scriptures, but they have taken good care to counteract its manifestly *Protestant tone*, by appending a large addition of Papal comment.

They have never dared to give the pure word of God to the people. What would you think if Presbyterians and Methodists should refuse to publish a Bible, unless interlarded with Calvanistic or Armenian comments? Would you not say that they were afraid of the Bible? This Romish version of the Scriptures is called the Douay Bible, because made at a town of that name in France. Every scholar knows that it is a poor affair compared with our common English Bible, and that it contains many gross inaccuracies. Nor could it well be otherwise. The version of the Bible in common use among the Protestants, was made in England, under the reign of King James, in the year 1611. It was a careful translation of the original Greek and Hebrew, made by a large number of wise and good men. The Douay Bible is a translation of the Latin Vulgate, not of the Greek and Hebrew. It is a translation of a translation. This Latin Vulgate is itself a mixed and imperfect affair. I will simply mention one gross mistranslation, as a specimen of the rest. We frequently meet with the word repentance in the New Testament. It is a translation of the Greek word *Metanoia*, and expresses one of the conditions of salvation. It is a very important word. In the Douay Bible it is translated, *doing penance*. For this translation there is no earthly warrant. They might as well have rendered it *dance a jig*. Dr. Nevins justly remarks : " It would seem as if they were anxious to avoid the use of any word which expressed or implied either *sorrow* or *amendment*, and therefore they fix on the phrase *doing penance*. I am mistaken if these translators have not a solemn account to give. This single rendering, if it were the only exceptionable one, would be as a millstone about the neck of that translation. Just think of the false impression, and that on a point of the highest moment, made on the minds of so many millions by this one egregiously erroneous version."—*Thoughts on Popery*, page 113. But the Church of Rome does not want the people to have the word of God in any form: and does not even look with favor on the general circulation and reading of the Douay Bible. As many may at first be tempted to question this statement we will go to a Romish work for proof, and once more appeal to the "End of Controversy." "Hence the Catholic Church requires her pastors, who are to preach and expound the word of God, to study this second part of her rule no less than the first part, with unremitting diligence; *and she encourages those of her flock, who are properly qualified and disposed, to read it for their edification.*" Notice two things, first, reading the Bible is not required as a Christian duty. It is merely *encouraged.* Second, only a few can ever enjoy this privilege: "*those who are properly qualified and disposed.*" This extract may be found on the 99th page of Dr. Milner's celebrated work. But again he tells us that: " The Catholic clergy must, and do employ, no small portion of their time, every day, in reading different portions of holy writ. But no such obligation is generally incumbent on the flock, that is, on the laity; it is sufficient for them to hear the word of God from those whom God has appointed to announce and explain it to them, whether by sermons, or catechisms, or other good books, or in the tribunal of penance." Page 311.

This does not look as though Rome favored much the free circulation and reading of the Bible. But history gives us additional facts. In the 11th century, Pope Gregory VII. (the patron saint of American bishops) formerly returned thanks to God, because the decadence of the Latin tongue made the old Latin Bible unfamiliar to the people. In 1229, the Council of Toulouse in its 14th canon "forbids the laity to have in their possession any copy of the books of the Old and New Testament, except the Psalter, and such portions of them as are contained in the Breviary, or the Hours of the Virgin: and most strictly forbids these works in the vulgar tongue." The Council of Tarracone, 1242, ordered all versions of the Bible, that were in the language of the people, to be brought to the bishops and burnt. In the "Ten Rules Concerning Prohibited Books," drawn up by order of the Council of Trent, and approved by Pope Pius IV., we find in rule III. that versions of the Old Testament may be "allowed only to pious and learned men at the discretion of the Bishop." In rule IV. the free circulation of the Bible is declared to be hurtful in the extreme; permission to read it must be obtained of the bishop or inquisitor, and all booksellers selling it to unauthorized persons are to be punished.

The position of Rome on this subject has never changed. In 1816, 1832, and 1824, ordinances were issued from the Papal throne, against the diffusion of the pure Word of God. In the August number of the *Catholic World* for the year 1868, the burning of Protestant translations of the Holy Bible is boldly justified. Enough has been said to show that the Church of Rome is the deadly foe of the Bible. As Protestants, we are prepared to boldly announce that we will never give up our right to read and study the Bible for ourselves. We will have it in our public shools, in our families and in our churches. It is too precious a book to be easily given up. Rome had better beware how she touches this, the *Magna Charta* of our spiritual freedom. We live in a Bible land, and in a Bible age.

CHAPTER V.

THE TEST APPLIED.

"*Ye shall know them by their fruits.*"—MATT. vii., 16.
"*Out of thine own mouth will I judge thee.*"—LUKE xix., 22.

MEN may use the same term, but yet attach to it a widely different meaning. There are few words in our language employed in so many different ways, as the word "Church." Roman Catholics differ widely from Protestants in their view of the Church of Christ. Romanists claim that Jesus Christ established a visible ecclesiastical organization, in communion with which salvation is certain—out of which, it is impossible. We do not deny the existence of a visible church, but claim that "The Church (or a part of it) is there where the word and the sacraments are; and the society in which the one is preached, and the other administered is a legitimate part of the visible Catholic Church."—*Litten on the Church, page* 254.

Of this visible church very wicked men may become members. The wheat and tares grow together. It is clear, then, that the true Church of Christ on earth must be invisible in its nature, and can only include those who love the Lord Jesus in sincerity and in truth. Such we claim it to be. The marks of the true Church as given by most Roman Catholic writers are unity, sanctity, catholicity and apostolicity. These they claim belong to the Church of Rome; hence it is the true, the only Church. We maintain that these attributes can only be found in the invisible Church, and that no visible corporation or society on earth has ever been endowed with them. Least of all do they belong to the Church of Rome. This we propose to show; and thus judging Rome by her own standard, we shall condemn her out of her own mouth. The first testing attribute set up by Rome, is that of unity. On this theme they never seem weary of harping. Our church, say they, is ever the same—the same in government, the same in doctrine, and the same in worship—the same in every age and in every land: while Protestants are divided up into a vast number of discordant and hostile sects. This boast, however, has but little foundation in fact. The simple truth is, that change after change has taken place in the government and worship of the church; one doctrine after another has been added to the faith, while between the various monastic orders and parties, there has been far more difference and hostility than exists between the various denominations of Protestantism.

Suppose we look first at the matter of government. The Pope is the great central power in Romanism—hence, it is very properly called Popery. He is the vicar of Christ, the Head of the Church, and in illustration of his supposed power over three worlds—Heaven, Earth and Hell—wears a triple crown. What can be more important in the government of the church than the manner of electing a Pope? Well, suppose it can be shown that the Church of Rome has greatly varied in the manner of selecting the successors of St. Peter, will it not look bad for the boasted unity? Let us take Maimbourg, the great Jesuit historian, for our guide. We do this that our opponents may not charge us with unfairness. According to Maimbourg, the first Pope selected his own successor. Then for the next five centuries, sometimes the people alone, sometimes the clergy alone, and sometimes the people and clergy conjointly, elected a Pope by a plurality of votes. Here are five different ways of choosing a Head for the Church. Then for the next twenty years no Pope could be chosen without the consent of the reigning prince. By and by, the Gothic kings cut the matter short by selecting the Pontiff without consulting either people or clergy. At the present time, the Pope is elected by the College of Cardinals: but we might show by continuing our study of this Jesuit historian, that before the present manner of selecting a Pope was fixed upon, there have been thirty fundamental variations in this important matter. Another curious reflection must come in right here. In 1181 the cardinals began to assume the sole power of electing a Pope. For eleven centuries they had no voice whatever in the election of a Pope. For the last five centuries they have had all to say in the matter. For eleven centuries those whom Christ appointed to select his representative had no voice in that election; or for more than five centuries those whom Christ never called to this authority have taken violent possession of it, and thrust out the true electors. Alas, for us poor divided Protestants! We have no trouble in selecting a head for the church. We all agree that Christ is the great Head of the church. But not only has there been great difference among Romanists in the manner of selecting a head for the church, but there has often been no small amount of trouble in ascertaining who the real head was. Any one at all acquainted with church history has heard of the *great western schism*. Gregory XI. died in the year 1378. From that time until the year 1447, there were always two, and at one time three rival popes. One party had a Pope reigning in Rome, and the other party had a Pope reigning in Avignon.

This bears rather heavily on the unity argument. Another startling fact remains to be mentioned: Not only has the church had two and even three heads at a time, but more than once has had no head whatever. After the death of Pope Leo IX., the papal throne was vacant for an entire year. After the death of Nicholas IV., it was without an occupant for two years and three months; and again stood empty after the death of Benedict XI. for eleven months. Many other such cases might be mentioned. We have referred to the great western schism. It may be well to state that of this schism Maimbourg says: "It was the *twenty-ninth* which separated the Catholic communion, and *divided between different heads* the same church, to which, by all laws, human and divine, there should have been but one, and that in one person." *Glorious Unity.* In fact, the Church of Rome is *without a head every time a Pope dies*, for there is always an interval before another Pope can be elected.

Can it be that Christ's true church can sometimes have three or four heads at once, and then again have no head whatever? We Protestants think that the church can have but one head, and that that head is Christ Jesus, the ever living and ever blessed Saviour of men.

Which of the two beliefs do you regard as the most sensible? We have spoken of the change that has come over the government of the Romish Church; let us now look at the doctrines of this church and see if there has been any change there. The great strength of the Roman Catholic Church lies in its supposed infallibility. Yet strange to say, never before the decree of the late Ecumenical Council, have the Romish theologians been able to locate this infallibility. Some have placed it in the general council with the Pope at the head, while a few have ascribed it to the Pope alone. Archbishop Purcell, in his celebrated controversy with Alexander Campbell, distinctly repudiated any belief in the infallibility of the Pope alone. Dr. Milner, in his book on the papal controversy, distinctly says that no member of the Roman Catholic Church is required to believe in the individual infallibility of the Pope. Yet it has just been defined as a dogma, and those who refuse to believe it are pronounced anathema.

It is extremely difficult to see how this decree has any logical force. If the Council is fallible, why may it not err in pronouncing the Pope to be infallible? If the Pope pronounces himself to be infallible, we are then in a most ridiculous circle. *The Pope is infallible because he declares himself so ; and his declaration is true because he is infallible.* Such is the sublime logic of Rome. Take the dogma of the immaculate conception of the Virgin Mary. This was never required or defined as an article of faith until December 8th, 1854. Dr. Milner, writing in the beginning of the present century, said of it: "The church does not decide the controversy concerning the conception of the Blessed Virgin, and several other disputed points, because she sees nothing absolutely clear and certain concerning them, either in the written or the unwritten word, and therefore leaves her own children to form their own opinions concerning them." But if any one should now dare to speak or write against the dogma of the immaculate conception, he would at once be given over to endless damnation. This quotation from Dr. Milner is interesting, because it admits that there are "controversies" and "disputed points" even in the church claiming never to vary in the slightest particular. How can Romish writers claim the attribute of unity for a church, the history of which is a history of successive corruption and change?

The Apocrypha, and Vulgate, and tradition were not exalted to canonical authority until the sixteenth century. The use of the Latin tongue in worship to the exclusion of the vernacular, was introduced in the seventh century. Transubstantiation was first taught in the eighth century and made no small commotion. In the eleventh, the Lord's Supper was mutilated by the establishment of communion in one kind. In the twelfth, the doctrine of Seven Sacraments was first taught. The doctrines of the meritorious virtue of penance, of purgatory, and prayers for the dead, date no earlier than the seventh century, and were not positively affirmed until the year 1140. The power of granting indulgences was not claimed by the popes till the twelfth century. Auricular confession was first enjoined by the fourth Lateran Council, in the thirteenth century. The celibacy of the clergy as universal and compulsory was ordained at the end of the fourth, and was confirmed by Gregory VII. at the end of the eleventh century.

We admit that Romanism forms a single organization, but the secret of this is very simple. Every rebellious and offending member is at once cut off. Those who bow not to every papal dogma, are immediately given over to the awful fate of unruly heretics. Yet even after all this ecclesiastical pruning and carving, many elements of discord remain. The Romish Church is made up to a large extent of different orders and societies. These are united enough so far as opposition to and persecution of Protestants are concerned, yet are far from constituting a " happy family" among themselves. History acquaints us with long and bitter contests between the Franciscans and the Dominicans. The Jesuits have often been complained of to head-quarters, and were abolished by Clement XIV., in 1773, but restored by Pius VI., in 1814. There is now no small amount of discord between the Gallican and the Ultramontain parties. So much for the unity in the Roman Catholic Church. The second testing attribute or mark of the true church, claimed by Rome, is (do not laugh) *sanctity*. While absolute sanctity can only belong to the true invisible church, yet it is the design of pure religion to make men holy. " Be ye holy" is God's great command. " Without holiness no man shall see the Lord." A system of faith that works no change in the heart, and effects no reformation in the life, cannot be of God's devising. Now, we affirm of Romanism that it has even no tendency to make men holy. The fact that now and then we discover a saint within her pale, does not refute the charge, for isolated cases of moral rectitude have occurred even among the heathen. The Popes themselves have often been monsters in human form. This is admitted even by papal writers. The bishops and priests present a record, if possible, still darker. Says Dr. Ruter, in his Church History, speaking of the seventh century: "Almost every crime which disgraces humanity entered into the dark catalogue of clerical vices." The centuries that follow present no change, unless for the worse. Those who think that priestly morals have improved in modern times, would do well to consider the sad case of Edith O'Gorman: or the abduction of Mary Ann Smith, with its dark record of lies and forgery. These, some may say, are only spots upon the surface, yet they are dark and deep enough to reveal the corruption that must lurk within. If any reader of this book doubts the charge of corrupt teaching and practice, let him obtain and peruse *Den's Theology*, or the *Secreta Monita* of the Jesuits. Some parts of the former work are so obscene, that no publisher dare give them to the world in an English form. He would be subject to indictment under the law against indecent literature. The *Secreta Monita* contains the secret laws and regulations of the Society of Jesus or Jesuits, and form an exhibition of depravity and hellish teachings, absolutely appalling to contemplate. What can we expect from such teachers and such teaching? "Like priest, like people." "If the blind lead the blind, both shall fall into the ditch." The most degraded and depraved of our populace are in open and full communion with the boasted "Mother Church." And never does Rome elevate in the mental or moral scale, those who throng her altars. Of this we see the proof every day. It is safe to affirm that one-third of the crime committed in this country, is committed by Roman Catholics.

The history of the Romish Church is one long, dark record of bloodshed, oppression, hypocrisy and wrong. And to-day, there is no sign of any change for the better: no manifestations of spiritual life. It is still mumbling the misty traditions of the past, still encircled in medieval shadows, and still pouring forth a stream of corrupt teaching, that bears death and desolation on every poisoned wave. Hear the testimony of one who has recently drank of this stream, and tested by a sad experience the present spiritual condition of Romanism. Rev. Edward Husband, who left the Church of England for the Church of Rome, recently came back again, and in a public letter states some of his experiences during his sojourn among the Romanists. "*Wherever* I went I was forced by what *I saw and heard* to make a comparison between the individual spirituality of mind in those I had left behind me in the Anglican Catholic Church, and those I found in the Roman Catholic Church. The result was that I knew there was *far more* spirituality, *far more* personal piety, *far more* holiness amongst the members of the Church of England than amongst those of the Church of Rome. And this was (in the first instance) not the fault of individuals, but of the system in which they were being educated. They had certain forms and ceremonies to keep and perform, and they did them because it was their duty to do them: and when they had accomplished this duty, they flattered themselves that all was right in the sight of God. They worshiped him with their lips, but in too many cases their hearts were far from him. During the four or five months I was a Roman Catholic, I hardly ever heard the name Jesus devotionally mentioned. It was always the name of Our Lady. She was the '*Refugiam peccatoriam,*' not Christ, to the Roman Catholic in practice, though I hope in theory that it may be otherwise. Their churches, instead of sounding out the sweet name of Jesus, rang with the holy name of Mary: until her name, which, as a member of the Church of England, I loved and honored so highly, became shorn of nearly all its attractiveness because of the frightful abuse to which it was subjected. I never felt my soul so stirred and fired with indignation as when I saw the glory and supremacy of our only Saviour Jesus trampled upon by the Mariolatry of Rome. In short, it was the sense that I had left Jesus behind me (so to speak) in the Church of England, that drove me to her communion again. I felt that Mary, with all her blessedness, was a poor, poor exchange for the unfathomable love of Jesus. And search where I would, I could not find him in the devotions of the Roman Catholic Church, except in the background."

If sanctity is an attribute of the true church, surely the Church of Rome will have a difficult task in making good her high claims. The third mark of the true church given by Romish writers is that of Catholicity or universality. "Ours is the Catholic, that is, the universal church, therefore it must be the true one," is their great argument. This attribute does indeed belong to the true invisible Church of Christ. We are all one in him. But this true church has no one community on earth, and has no one visible ruler. The Romish Church proudly claims the title "Catholic" for herself, and thus assumes the very point in discussion. But if universal, why does she not include us? How is it, that beyond her pale, there are millions of truly pious souls, serving God, and working to extend his Kingdom? The lives of these are, at least, as holy, their word as good, and their deaths as peaceful as though they were in communion with the Church of Rome. The Church of Rome is no more entitled to the name Catholic, than the Greek Church, the Church of England, or the Methodist Episcopal Church. A part cannot be the whole. But let our opponents speak for themselves. " The true church is Catholic: or Universal in three several respects: as to *persons*, as to *places*, and as to *time*. It consists of *the most numerous body of Christians;* it is more or less *diffused, wherever Christianity prevails:* and it has *visibly existed ever since the time of the apostles.*"—*End of Controversy, page* 179.

Let us look at the three points named: First, the Romish Church is Catholic, because it consists of the " most numerous body of Christians." *In other words it consists of the* " *most numerous body of Christians,*" *therefore it includes all the Christians. Glorious logic! Second, it is more or less diffused wherever Christianity prevails.* But the same may be said of the Presbyterian, Baptist, or Methodist Episcopal Church. We are all "more or less diffused wherever Christianity prevails:" and are pushing out daily into regions where it does not prevail. Third, "it has visibly existed ever since the time of the apostles." In the second chapter of this book, the reader will find this point examined. It has there been shown that Romanism is a great apostacy, a gradual corruption of Christian truth. The apostles knew as little about the teachings of Romanism, as Romanists seem to know about the teachings of the apostles. The last testing attribute set up by Roman Catholics is that of *Apostolicity*. They mean by this that their Popes form an unbroken succession from the days of Peter to the present time, and that no man has any right to exercise sacred functions, unless he derives his commissions through the Papal See. In proof of this they exhibit a curious list of the Popes, beginning with St. Peter and ending with Pius IX. We intend in a future chapter to give this subject a full discussion. Let it suffice to remark here that except to a few high-churchmen in the Church of England and Protestant Episcopal

Church in this country, this boasted apostolic chair is a universal laughing stock. John Wesley was for many years inclined to high-church views: but after a careful investigation of the subject, he was compelled to admit that "*Apostolic Succession is a fiction which no man ever did or can prove.*" But on this subject more anon. Rome is thus condemned by her own assumptions. We can turn her weapons against her, and by the tests that she lays down, show that she is not the true Church of Christ.

CHAPTER VI.

THE GREAT USURPER.

"Who opposeth and exalteth himself above all that is called God, or that is worshiped; so that he as God sitteth in the temple of God, shewing himself that he is God." — 2 THES. ii., 4.

EVERY system of faith has its great central head: the source from which it emanates, and the recognized authority in all matters of dispute. Romanism has such a central head. What Christ is to the Christian, Mohammed to the believer in the Koran, Brahma to the Hindoo, or Brigham Young to the Mormon, the Pope is to the Roman Catholic. His devotion is directed to Rome rather than to Bethlehem or Calvary. The power of the Pope in spiritual matters is regarded as supreme: and as the interests of the soul are superior to the interests of the body, he is supposed by many Romanists to have supreme power over states and princes.

He is the great Head of the Church, and from his infallible teaching there can be no appeal. He is the Vicar of Christ, and carries the keys of Heaven and Hell. He is called by the most blasphemous of titles, blasphemous because they belong of right only to Diety: and is approached with the most abject adoration. His blessing is sought as the greatest of boons, while his curse is supposed to convey unnumbered woes. Such are the views, and such the practice of the Romish Church on this subject.

It is well known that these enormous claims of power and dominion, are built up on the supposed supremacy of St. Peter, and on the assumption that each reigning Pope is his direct successor. We propose to show that Peter neither claimed nor exercised any supremacy over the other disciples: and that if he did, the Pope cannot prove that he is his successor. The passage on which Romanists base their high claims for the Papacy is Matt. xvi., 18–19. "And I say unto thee, That thou art Peter, and upon this rock I will build my church, and the gates of

Hell shall not prevail against it. And I will give unto thee the keys of the Kingdom of Heaven; and whatsoever thou shalt bind on earth, shall be bound in Heaven; and whatsoever thou shalt loose on earth shall be loosed in Heaven." On this text the entire superstructure of Papal dominion has been erected. The keys and the rock is their unfailing argument. From the bold and decided manner in which they continually quote these words, one would not be led to suppose that the argument derived from them and the false meaning ascribed to them, had been exposed and refuted a thousand times. Yet, such is the fact. We must use Scripture to explain Scripture. A concordance is often better than a commentary. The verses preceding the text in dispute, furnish a key to its successful interpretation.

"When Jesus came into the coasts of Cesarea Phillippi, he asked his disciples, saying: Whom do men say that I, the Son of Man, am? And they said: Some say that thou art John the Baptist; some Elias, and others Jeremiah, or one of the prophets. He saith unto them, But whom say ye that I am? And Simon Peter answered and said: Thou art the Christ, the Son of the living God. And Jesus answered and said unto him: Blessed art thou, Simon Bar-jona, for flesh and blood hath not revealed it unto thee, but my Father which is in heaven. And I say unto thee, that thou art Peter," etc. Now, *what is the rock?* All hinges on this. Is it Peter, or the glorious confession of our Lord's Divinity, that Peter had just made? We think that it is the latter.

1. The Greek word *petros* or Peter does not mean a rock, but a stone, or little piece of a rock; but *petra* (of which our Lord says, "Upon this *petra* I will build my church,") does mean a rock. Now a real rock is superior to a mere stone, or a little piece of the rock. Again, *petros* is a masculine noun, but *petra* is feminine. How then can Peter be referred to as the rock on which the church is built? He cannot be the rock, and yet only a small piece of the rock at the same time.

2. Christ is, in other passages, expressly declared to be the foundation or rock on which the church is built. "For other foundation can no man lay than that is laid, which is Christ Jesus." 1 Cor. iii., 11.

3. A rock implies courage and immovability, when employed as a metaphor: but Peter was proverbially impulsive and fickle. The gates of hell so far prevailed against him, that he denied his Master with oaths and curses. Through fear of the Jews, he also refused to mingle at Antioch with the Gentile converts, and was openly withstood to the face by Paul. "Because he was to be blamed." So much for the rock. Now, what about the keys? Why, our Lord gave them to Peter. The Bible says so, and that is enough for us Protestants. "And I will give unto thee the keys of the Kingdom of Heaven." This is one of the few passages that Roman Catholics are willing to admit is easy to be understood. But, what are keys for? Why, to unlock and open a door is one of the uses to which they may be put; and the only other use that I ever heard of is to lock

it again. Well, to which use did Peter put the keys? "He opened the Kingdom of Heaven, that is, the Gospel Church, or Christian dispensation, to both Jews and Gentiles. He preached the first sermon, and was the instrument of making the first converts among each. With one key he opened the Kingdom of Heaven to the Jews, and with the other to the Gentiles. This was a distinction conferred on Peter, it is true; but it was necessary that some one of the twelve should *begin* the business of preaching the Gospel. The whole twelve could not turn the keys and open the doors."—*Nevins on Popery, page* 45. But who has the power of the keys now? Why no one. What could they do with the keys if they had them? Peter opened the door, and it is never to be closed. If a door is unlocked and opened, and is never to be shut again, who cares what becomes of the keys? But Roman Catholics say that those keys signify the authority conferred on the Church, and especially on the Popes. The keys have been passed along from one to another, until they have reached old Pius

IX., making each Pope the door-keeper of heaven. But where is the Scripture warrant for such claims? Simply, nowhere. We challenge any one to find it. Christ will attend to that matter himself. "He that hath the key of David, he that openeth and no man shutteth, and shutteth and no man openeth," is not the Pope, but Christ.—Rev. iii., 7.

So much for the keys. The poor Pope can get no more comfort from them than he does from the rock. Now, one more point remains to be considered, namely: the power of binding and loosing. This power was conferred on Peter, it is true; but not on him alone. It was conferred on the entire twelve. In Matt. xviii., 18, Christ addressed them as a body, and says: "Verily I say unto you, whatsoever ye shall bind on earth shall be bound in heaven; and whatsoever ye shall loose on earth, shall be loosed in heaven." The meaning of this declaration is not difficult to understand. In the Jewish language, to bind and loose were words made use of by the Rabbi; to signify the lawfulness or unlawfulness of things. Whatsoever, then, the disciples, as the inspired teachers of the Church, should declare to be forbidden to men on the earth, should be forbidden by heaven, and whatsoever they should permit to be done, should be lawful in the sight of heaven. This power, however, belongs only to the apostles, and no more to Peter than to all the rest. Peter never claimed any supremacy over his brethren. He suffered himself to be openly rebuked by Paul. He wrote two encyclical or general epistles; but they bear no resemblance to those issued by Pius IX., or any other of those claiming to be St. Peter's successors.

He commences his epistle "Peter, an Apostle of Jesus Christ." Why, what is the matter with the man? He claims no supremacy whatever over his brethren, for Paul frequently began his epistles in the same way. Why does he not say, "Peter, Primate of the Apostolical College, Supreme and Infallible Head of the Church," etc.? This would be somewhat in the style of a modern Pope. But in the first verse of the fifth chapter of his first letter, we find a still stronger declaration: "The elders which are among you I exhort, who am also an elder." I do not wonder that while the letters and speeches of Pius IX. may be read by any one, the two letters of Peter (Pope Peter, they would say,) cannot be read by a Roman Catholic layman, without the addition of notes and comments. I do not wonder that while the letters and bulls of Pius IX. may be understood by anybody, that while private interpretation is allowed here, the church and tradition can alone explain the letters of poor Peter. But Peter was inspired by the Holy Ghost. All admit this. To what conclusion then are we driven? Why, that Peter with inspiration, is a poorer and more careless writer than Pius IX. and all other Popes are without it! What an absurd and blasphemous doctrine.

We are not through with this matter of the first Pope yet. *Peter was married.* This is bad for a Pope. Not even a common priest in the Romish Church, dare take a wife. But there can be no mistake about the case of Peter. The New Testament tells us that his wife's mother was very ill with a fever, and that Jesus *restored her to health.* If she had only died, there would have been no trouble. I wonder if Roman Catholics do not wish that she had died. Romanists tell us that Peter did not live with his wife, after he became Pope: but the Bible gives us no such intelligence. The Roman Catholic Church tells us that it is indebted to tradition for this precious piece of information. Now, it is very nice to have tradition to appeal to. It is such a dim, shadowy thing, that if it were asserted that tradition teaches us that the moon is made of green cheese, it would be difficult to directly disprove it. But we Protestants are cruel enough to fling tradition aside, and keep the discussion centered around the Bible. Peter then was a married man, and lived with his wife like a respectable Christian. Some may be unreasonable enough to think that this is much better, than to live as many of the Popes have done, in sinful relation to the wives of others. You see when a man leaves the infallible church, there is no telling what queer notions he may entertain. Again, the Pope must reside at Rome: but we have no good reason to believe that Peter ever saw the city of Rome. The Bible tells us nothing about it. So they fall back on *tradition* again. Tradition says that Peter was Bishop of Rome, and that he died in that city. In the words of an eminent author, we think that: "Tradition must be treated as a notorious liar, to whom we give no credit, unless what he says is confirmed by some one in whom we can rely. If it be affirmed by him alone, we must suspend our belief until we obtain better testimony." The story of Peter's visit to Rome is mixed up with so much absurdity, as to utterly destroy our faith in the whole transaction. We are told, for instance, that he went there chiefly to oppose Simon, the magician. That at their first meeting, Simon flew up into the air, in the sight of the whole city: that the Devil, frightened by the name of Jesus, let him fall to the ground, by which fall he broke his legs, and so on, *ad nauseum*. They will show you to-day in Rome, the place where Peter kneeled on the occasion, and a stone marked with the blood of Simon. We must receive a hundred such stories, if we admit Peter to have been at Rome, for they all rest on the same authority. We will conclude what we have to say on the supremacy of Peter, by adducing some more Scripture testimony on the subject. We deem this a better guide than tradition. We read of a strife among the apostles as to who among them should be greatest. "And there was also a strife among them, which of them should be accounted the greatest. And he said unto them, the kings of the Gentiles exercise lordship over them; and they that exercise authority upon them are called benefactors. But ye shall not be so: but he that is greatest among you, let him be as the younger, and he that is chief as he that doth serve." (Luke xxii., 24, 25, 26.) Three questions at once occur, which we will leave Romanists to answer. First, if our Lord, by the figure of the rock and keys, had just given the supremacy to Peter, why should there be any dispute among the apostles, as to who should be chief? Second, why did not our Lord answer plainly that Peter should be chief, if such was his design? Third, how does the statement of our Lord, as to the lack of lordship and authority among the disciples, agree with the claims of the Papacy?

Several events in the history of the early Christian Church, as recorded in the Acts of the Apostles, are very difficult to understand, if Peter was the first Pope.

First, Peter in company with John, was sent to the newly converted Church in Samaria by the other apostles. " Now when the apostles which were at Jerusalem heard that Samaria had received the Word of God, they sent unto them Peter and John."—Acts viii., 14.

This looks bad for Peter's supremacy. *He must have forgotten about the keys.*

Second, The Church did not receive with unquestioned faith the teaching of Peter.

On the contrary: " When Peter was come up to Jerusalem, they that were of the circumcision contended with him, saying: Thou wentest in to men uncircumcised, and didst eat with them.

But Peter rehearsed the matter from the beginning, and expounded it by order unto them."—Acts xi., 2–4. This looks worse yet. They "contended" with Peter. Now, surely, he will flourish the keys, and fall back on infallibility. Not a bit of it. He does not even pronounce them "*Anathema*," but "rehearsed the matter from the beginning, and expounded it by order unto them." Well, they certainly had better success than some of their fellow-heretics in after ages. Poor Luther was excommunicated, Huss was burned, the body of Wickliff was dug up and given to the flames, and all for "contending" with those who claim to be the literal successors of St. Peter.

Third, The first General Council of the Church was held at Jerusalem. Peter made a speech, but James presided, and pronounced the decision. See the fifteenth chapter of Acts. Verily, the Bible *is* a hard book to understand, if we must reconcile it to the claims and teachings of Romanism. "Let us hear the conclusion of the whole matter."

First, Christ never declared Peter to have any supremacy over his brethren.

Second, Peter never claimed or exercised any such supremacy; for he simply calls himself an apostle and elder, suffered Paul to openly withstand him, allowed the Church to call in question his teaching, was *sent* by his brethren to Samaria, and did not preside in the Council in Jerusalem.

Third, He was a married man.

Fourth, We have no reason to believe that he ever saw the city of Rome, much less established there the Papal See.

Fifth, The power claimed for him and his supposed successors by the Romish Church, is in direct conflict with the teachings of our Saviour as to the spiritual nature of his Kingdom, and the purity of his ministers.

We now propose to show that even if Peter did have any supremacy over his brethren, it cannot be proved that the Popes are his successors. This can soon be done. We are well aware that a long list of Popes, extending from

Peter to Pius IX., is exhibited in triumph by the Romish Church. This *looks* very convincing. If naughty Protestants only *would* cease to question and examine everything, and trust to tradition and the Infallible Church — there would be no more trouble. What is the use of infallibility if you have to stop and prove everything? They might as well be without it. Suppose we look at this boasted chain a little. Somehow we have contracted a very bad habit of looking into matters and things for ourselves, and feel very little fear of papal curses. One thing must be remembered about this chain. To be of any value it must be complete. If a single link is broken, the chain is of no more use. Well, then, if Peter was the first Pope, who succeeded him? Who was the second Pope? *St. Clement*, say some; *St. Linus*, say others. All start off with Peter, but the very next step is uncertain. The fathers do not agree about it. Turtullian says that St. Clement succeeded Peter; while other fathers bestow this honor on St. Linus. Now, we cannot, according to the Church of Rome, explain a single passage of the Scripture, unless we have the unanimous consent of the holy fathers. Now, suppose we apply the same rule to this papal chain. It is a poor rule that will not work in more than one way. Have not things come to a pretty pass? The very first link in this chain is broken. No one can tell who was the second Pope. We might go on and show that the way grows darker and darker as we advance; but we will wait until they find the "missing link." It might seem cruel to keep up the investigation. The Church of Rome has a doctrine called "intention," that casts a still deeper gloom about this chain. If in administering a sacrament, the administrator intends to bestow the grace, it is accomplished, no matter what the character of the recipient. If, on the other hand, the administrator does not intend to bestow the grace, it is withheld, in the same strange and arbitrary manner. Now, suppose we knew that St. Clement and not St. Linus, or St. Linus and not St. Clement, succeeded St. Peter; suppose the historic character of this famous chain is all right, how are we to know that each reigning Pope was a literal successor of St. Peter? For if in ordaining a Pope, the administrator did not *intend* to ordain, the matter was not accomplished, and the poor man was no Pope after all. This makes "confusion worse confounded." It has been shown in a previous chapter that the boasted succession has frequently been interrupted by vacations and schisms. It has frequently been decreed by councils, that all those ordinations are null and void, in which the person to be ordained secured his elevation by fraud or bribery. Now, we know that the popedom has often been obtained by just such unfair means. Here, then, is another way in which succession has been interrupted. According to the Romish doctrine, no heretic can transmit episcopal or priestly power to another. This looks bad for the succession, as many of the Popes have been heretics. Pope Libreius was an Arian; Anastasius was a Nestorian; Honorius was a Monothelite; John XX. taught that the souls of the pious, when released from the body, would not see God before the Day of Judgment; John XXIII. believed that the soul died with the body. This is affirmed of him by the Council of Constance. Many of the Popes have been men of the vilest character.

Can we believe that God would call such men to preside over his Church, and teach his truth? *Monstrous!* Roman Catholics themselves admit that one-tenth of the Popes have disgraced the office. Alas for this boasted chain! It is broken at a hundred points, and all covered with rust and blood. Well has Bishop Janes said : " He who would trace his ecclesiastical pedigree up to the chair of Peter, must wade through slime and blood to his very neck." We will now conclude what we have to say on this branch of the subject, by summing up our reasons for refusing to believe in this boasted succession.

1. The list of reigning Popes presented by the Church of Rome has no historic value.

2. The successions has been interrupted by long and repeated vacations.

3. And also by violent and frequent schisms.

4. According to the doctrine of "intention," many of those occupying the papal throne, may never have been ordained to the office.

5. Many of the Popes have been heretics, and according to the Romish Church, no heretic can properly transmit priestly or episcopal power.

6. Many of the Popes have obtained the office by fraud and bribery; and this, according to the views of our opponents, is enough to render their ordination void.

7. Many of the Popes have been men of vile character.

CHAPTER VII.

THE MASS.

"*Teaching for doctrines the commandments of men.*"—MATT. xv., 9.

HAVING cleared away the false rules of faith and practice, adopted by the Romish Church, and established our right to read and understand the Bible, and argue from it alone: having shown by their own tests, that the Romish corporation is not the true Church of Christ, and demonstrated the unreliable nature of their boasted succession: we are now prepared to examine their false teachings and corrupt doings in the light of God's holy word. We will begin with what they are pleased to term the *Mass*. The word is not in the Bible. They had to invent it. If you went to one of their churches when they were celebrating mass, you would hardly think that it was intended to represent the humble scene in the little upper chamber at Jerusalem, or in other words, that it was the *Lord's Supper.* True, they have the bread (in the form of a wafer, but we let that pass,) and the wine: but here the resemblance ceases. They, however, do not regard it as bread and wine; but as the *body and blood, soul and divinity* of the Lord Jesus Christ. This they *eat and drink.* Surely, this must be a Protestant misrepresentation. No, here it is in the catechism:

" *Q.* What is the holy eucharist? *A.* It is a sacrament, which contains the body and blood, soul and divinity of Jesus Christ, under the forms and appearance of bread and wine.

" *Q.* Is it not bread and wine which is first put upon the altar for the celebration of mass? *A.* Yes; it is always bread and wine till the priest pronounces the words of consecration during mass.

" *Q.* What happens by these words? *A.* The bread is changed into the body of Jesus Christ, and the wine into his blood.

" *Q.* What is this change called? *A.* It is

called transubstantiation, that is to say, a change of one substance into another."

This is the doctrine taught to every Roman Catholic child in the country. And all this is founded on the simple words of Jesus: "This is my body." True, he right after, called the wine, (which Romanists say is his blood) the "fruit of the vine;" and Paul in his first epistle to the Corinthians calls the bread, bread, and not the "body and blood, soul and divinity of Jesus Christ." True, Christ is in other places called a rock, a door, a vine, ("I *am* the door." "I *am* the vine." "That rock *was* Christ,") thus plainly showing that the words "this is my body," are to be taken figuratively; true, we can still see after the mystic words of consecration, that it is bread and wine, and not body and blood: but what are Scripture or reason when they conflict with the teaching of the Church of Rome? *The body of Christ* is *said to be entire in each particle of the sacred host.* To state this absurd and blasphemous doctrine is its best refutation. It is simply *incapable of belief.* Yet it has been called the *burning article* in the Church of Rome. Thousands have been burned and tortured because they would not believe it. But we are not through with the enormities of the mass. After professing to turn the bread and wine into Jesus Christ, (this is simply a shorter way of stating it) the priest claims to offer him up in sacrifice. This they call the "unbloody sacrifice of the mass." This is no Protestant slander. Read the canons of the Council of Trent on this subject:

"Canon 1. If any one shall say, that a true and proper sacrifice is not offered to God in the mass; or that what is to be offered is nothing else than giving Christ to eat; let him be accursed. Canon 2. If any one shall say, that by these words 'Do this for a commemoration of me,' Christ did not appoint his apostles priests, or did not ordain that they and other priests should offer his body and blood: let him be accursed."

Is not this in direct violation of the oft-made declaration of Scripture, that Jesus was *once* offered, and then completed the work of human redemption? Does it not give the *lie* to the dying words of Jesus? He declared that it was finished. Rome says, it has been going on ever since, and will continue to the end of time. Then "an *unbloody* sacrifice," does not agree very well with the declaration of Scripture that "without shedding of blood is no remission." Cain offered an "unbloody sacrifice," but there was no divine recognition of it. He went forth, however, to slay his brother, and so has Romanism, with its "unbloody sacrifice," more than once stained its altars with the blood of heretics.

According to the Romish doctrine Christ has been offered millions of times. A little, ignorant priest can cause the Saviour of the World to be offered whenever he pleases. The sacrifice on Calvary is not enough. We are prepared now to hear of almost any absurdity in connection with the mass; and need not wonder to hear that Roman Catholics worship the consecrated wafer. Yes, they actually fall down and worship it. The priest lifts it up to the people, and cries, "*Ecce Agnus Dei, qui tollit mundi peccata—Behold the Lamb of God, that taketh away the sin of the world.*" The congregation fall down and worship it, crying, "*Mea culpa, mea culpa, mea maxima culpa—My fault, my fault, my very great fault.*" Then they walk up and *eat it.* Do the very heathen go ahead of this? Did ever a heathen make a god, consecrate him, worship him, and then turn around and eat him? They tell us that it is not the wafer they worship, but that the wafer has been turned into the blessed Saviour. We have just shown that this is impossible. In fact, it needs no showing. There it is, still a wafer. *If we cannot believe our senses,* we *cannot believe anything.* They *think* that it is the blessed Saviour; but then that does not make it so, or exempt them from the charge of idolatry. All idolatry is founded on ignorance. This moreover is willful ignorance. All they have to do is to believe their senses.

One more folly remains to be considered in relation to this subject. The Church of Rome withholds the cup from the laity. This was done by the Council of Trent. All admit that before this, the laity communed in both kinds. Now the poor layman can only have half a sacrament, or really no sacrament whatever. It is true that Christ administered it in both kinds, and the early Church did the same, and we never hear of a divided sacrament before the Council of Trent; but what are these trifles to an Infallible Church? See what a vast change Romanism has made in the simple and beautiful sacraments of the Lord's Supper. Five fearful changes have been made.

First, The doctrine of transubstantiation has been invented.

Second, They pretend to offer up Christ.

Third, They use a wafer instead of bread.

Fourth, They worship this wafer.

Fifth, They withhold the cup from the laity.

Surely this is a terrible record. I would love to have two pictures painted and placed side by side: one representing the simple scene in the little upper chamber, when Christ instituted the Last Supper; and the other representing mass as performed in a Romish Church. We might well say, "Look on this picture, and then on that." I would love to see the man who could trace any connection or resemblance between the two. If this was the only corruption introduced by the Roman Catholic Church, it were enough to sink her forever, like a mill-stone, beneath the waves of the sea. But we shall find much more to excite holy indignation, ere we finish our investigation of her abominations.

CHAPTER VIII.

CONFESSION.

"*Every crime, as I have stated before, which the Romish Church sanctions, and almost all the immoralities of its members, either originate in or have some connection with Auricular Confession.*"—HOGAN.

IT is a peculiar feature in the economy of Romanism, that it perverts and misguides elements in human nature, that originally are good and beneficial. For instance, it is natural for a soul, when burdened beneath a load of sin and guilt, to confess this sin and misery, and to cry out, "God be merciful to me, a sinner." The Romish Church, at this point, comes in between the soul and its Saviour, and sends the trembling sinner to the priest; to him his sins must be confessed, and through him pardon must be received. All this sounds very strange to Protestant ears, yet it is the unchanging doctrine, and daily practice of the Roman Catholic Church. We prefer to state their doctrines in the language of their own standards, that none may charge us with unfairness or misrepresentation. It is difficult to state fairly the views of an opponent, unless you do it in his own language.

Well, here it is: "Whoever shall affirm that the confession of every sin, according to the customs of the Church, is impossible, and merely a human tradition, which the pious should reject; or that all Christians, of both sexes, are not bound to observe the same once a year, according to the constitution of the great Council of Lateran; and, therefore, that the faithful in Christ are to be persuaded not to confess in Lent, Let him be accursed."—*Council of Trent decrees.* Canon 8, *Sess.* xiv.

If these confessions were made to God, we would interpose no objection (though what man could recount and specify every sin that he had ever committed?); but they are made to a priest, a fellow-man, a *fellow-sinner*. We all admit that sin should be confessed; but common sense would indicate that the confession should be made to the Being offended. We do not read of any one in the Bible who confessed his sins to a priest; David confessed to God. "I acknowledge my sin unto thee, and mine iniquity have I not hid; I said, I will confess my transgressions unto the Lord, and thou forgavest the iniquity of my sin." — Psa. xxxii., 5. He adds, moreover: "For this (the forgiveness of sin) shall every one that is godly pray unto thee, in a time when thou mayest be found."

If David confessed to God, why not any other sinner? If Isaiah, Job, Daniel, Paul, Peter, and the poor publican confessed to God, why may not we? We object, then, to auricular confession, that it has no foundation in Scripture. We do not read that any of the apostles established a confessional. It has been said that we read of no one in the Bible, who confessed to a priest. We forgot about *Judas Iscariot.* He did not go to God with his confession, but to the chief priests. *He also took money,* thirty pieces of silver. We will not investigate the case of Judas any farther. The Romanists are welcome to all the comfort and support they can get from it. I know that the Romanists quote the well-known passage, "Confess your faults one to another;" but this implies something mutual. It bears not the smallest resemblance to confession as practiced in the Romish Church. Does the priest turn around and confess to his parishioners? If not, how can it be called confessing "one to another?" Auricular confession is an insult to Christ. He is the great, the *only* Mediator between God and man. Why, then, need the priest interfere? Christ says to men, "Come unto me;" but Rome says: "You must go to the priest; he is to you in the place of God." We object to Romish confession, that it is absurd.

I have not sinned against the priest, but against God. If a child should sin against his father, would he go to a neighbor with his confession; or to make the illustration stronger, would he go to a brother, who had sinned equally with himself? Suppose they confess to each other, and forgive each other, will that satisfy the father? Romanists tell us that parties must repent before they can obtain absolution; that the priest cannot forgive them until they do repent; well, if they sincerely repent, will not *God* forgive them, and then who cares whether the priest forgives or not? At the very best, auricular confession is useless. Facts, with which every one ought to be acquainted, compel us to urge another objection against confession. *It is immoral in its tendencies and results.* As Romanists stoutly deny this, and urge the contrary, we will take special pains to prove it. It produces immorality both in the confessor and in the confessed. It produces immorality in the confessor. The mind of the priest becomes a sink for the reception and retention of all sorts of moral corruption. He must listen month after month, and year after year, to the most disgusting details of all sorts of vice. Old men and children, young men and maidens, must pour into his attentive ear, a recital of their thoughts, desires, and most secret sins. This, surely, cannot have a very refining or sanctifying influence.

Then the secrets of the confessional must never be divulged. The priest must carry them forever in his own bosom. Rather than reveal anything made known in confession, he must stoop to lying and perjury. Here is the proof: Peter Den, in his Theology, which is the class-book in Maynooth College, in Ireland, and in other Romish schools, has the following, on the duty of confessions, in this respect: "*Can a case be given in which it is lawful to break the secrecy of the confession?* Answer: None can be given; although the life or salvation of a man, or the destruction of the commonwealth, would depend thereon. *What, then, ought a confessor to answer when interrogated respecting any truth which he knows only by sacramental confession?* Answer: He ought to answer that he does not know it; and, if necessary, to confirm that by an oath. *Obj. It is not lawful to lie in any case; but the confessor lies, because he knows the truth; therefore, he ought not to confirm by an oath that which is not true.* Ans. The minor proposition is denied; because such confessor is interrogated as a man, and answers as a man, but he does not know this truth as man, though he knows it as God."

Is not this beautiful morality? What must be the effect of such teaching and such practice on the minds of father confessors?

This confession to the priest, it must be remembered, is *not* a general one; but must all be given in detail. To do this, a long list of questions has been prepared. Each commandment (except the second, the Church of Rome has removed this from the decalogue, for reasons which we shall understand hereafter,) is gone over in turn. The most minute, and in some cases, disgusting questions are asked. I dare not pollute these pages with the list of questions asked on the sixth (our seventh) commandment. If the reader wishes to see them, he is referred to the " Garden of the Soul," a book published under the recommendation of the late Archbishop Hughes. This confession is always made in private, often by young and fair women, to men devoted by their ordination vows to a life of celibacy. The fair penitent kneels before the priest, a man of flesh, and blood, and passion. Her warm breath is upon his cheek. Into his ears she pours her most secret thoughts and desires. *Nothing must be concealed.* Could the devil himself invent anything better suited to ruin both soul and body? History is not silent on this subject: "In Spain, Pope Paul IV. uttered his bull against the crime of solicitants, or of those priests who, in the act of confession, solicit the person confessing to indecent acts. When this bull was introduced into Spain, every person who had been solicited was instructed, within thirty days, to report to the inquisitions. So great was the number of females who went to the palace of the inquisitor in the city of Seville only, to reveal the conduct of their infamous confessors, that twenty notaries, and as many inquisitors, were appointed to note down their several informations. But these being found insufficient, several periods of thirty days was appointed, and the matter was finally given up, and the whole matter terminated where it began."—*Elliott on Romanism, Vol. II., page* 323.

This is a picture of Romish morality as developed in the confessional, that may well make every lover of his land and his kind tremble with alarm.

I will conclude this branch of my subject by giving some extracts from the writings of the Rev. L. J. Nolan, once a popish priest, but now a Protestant minister: " During the last three years that I discharged the duties of a Romish clergyman, my heart often shuddered at the idea of entering the confessional. The thoughts of the many crimes I had to hear; the growing doubt upon my mind that confession was an erroneous doctrine, that it tended more to harden than to reclaim the heart, and that through it I should be rendered instrumental in ministering destruction to souls, were often considerations to me in the hours of my reflection. The recitals of the murderous acts I had often heard through this iniquitous tribunal, had cost me many a restless night, and are still fixed with horror in my memory. But the most awful of all consideration is this, that through the confessional I had been frequently *apprised of intended assassinations* and most diabolical conspiracies, and still from the ungodly injunctions of secrecy in the Romish creed, lest, as Peter Den says, 'the confessional should become odious,' I dared not give the slightest intimation to the marked-out victims of slaughter. But though my heart now trembles at the recollections of the murderous acts, still duty obliges me to proceed and enumerate one or two instances of the cases alluded to. The first is the case of a person who was barbarously murdered, and with whose intended assassination I became acquainted at confession. One of the five conspirators (all of whom were sworn to commit the horrid deed,) broached to me the bloody conspiracy in the confessional. I implored him to desist from his intentions of becoming an accomplice in so diabolical a design; but alas! all advice was useless, no dissuasion could prevail; his determination was fixed, and his only reason for having disclosed the awful machination to his confessor, seemed to have originated from *a hope that his wicked design would be hal-*

lowed by his previous acknowledgment of it to his priest. Finding all my remonstrances unavailing, I then recurred to stratagem. I earnestly besought him to mention the circumstances to me out of the confessional, in order that I might apprise the intended victim of his danger, or caution the conspirators against the committal of so inhuman a deed. But here ingenuity itself failed in arresting the career of his satanic obstinacy. The conspirator's illegal oath, and his apprehension of himself becoming the victim of brutal assassination, should he be known as the revealer of the conspiracy, rendered him inflexible to my entreaties; and awful to relate — yes, awful, and the hand that now pens it shudders at the record it makes — a poor, inoffensive man, the victim of slaughter, died a most cruel death by the hands of ruthless assassins."

Mr. Nolan then proceeds to relate a case still more heart-rending. All converted Romanists agree in regarding the confessional as the citadel of popish strength, and the great fountain of her moral corruption. It gives the priests and bishops an almost absolute control over the people. It is the chain that binds them to the throne of papacy. From early childhood, their most secret thoughts have been confided to the priests, the whole history of their lives have been committed to them, and shall they dare to rebel? May God in his mercy soon remove this great plague-spot from American soil.

CHAPTER IX.

PURGATORY.

"*To-day thou shalt be with me in paradise.*"—LUKE xxiii., 43.

"The saints who die of Christ possess'd,
  Enter into immediate rest;
For them no further test remains,
  Of purging fires and torturing pains."

C. Wesley.

YOU will not find the word "purgatory" in the Bible. Rome cannot express her doctrines and customs in scriptural language. She has been compelled to invent a terminology of her own. Mass, rosary, pope, extreme unction, chrism, acolyte, and a host of other words, very familiar to Romish ears, may be found in a dictionary, but not in the Bible. A "form of sound words" is of great value, but nevertheless, if the things themselves could only be found in the Word of God, we would not object so strongly to the use of new terms. But the worst of it is, that the doctrines and customs signified by these words, cannot be found in the Bible. Thus it is with the doctrine of purgatory. The Bible does not give it the faintest shadow of support. But what is this purgatory, about which we hear so much from Romanists, and of which we can find no trace in the Bible?

It is not Heaven. It is not Hell. They do not mean by it, the doctrine of the intermediate state, in which so many worthy Protestants believe, the place where departed spirits wait the resurrection from the dead, and the great day of judgment. They believe in purgatory as a place where the souls of departed Roman Catholics go to be purified and prepared for Heaven. It is not for Protestants. They must go direct to Hell. It is a place of *literal fire*, of *fearful pain*. Roman Catholic writers make its torments as great and terrible as are those of Hell. But then you may escape from purgatory, while in Hell there gleams no hope. This seems to be about the only difference. The escape from purgatory is helped and hastened by masses and prayers offered by the priests. Such is the Romish doctrine of purgatory. But we had better state it in their own language. In the creed drawn up by the Council of Trent, before quoted at length, it is stated thus: "I constantly hold that there is a purgatory, and that the souls therein detained are helped by the suffrages of the faithful." Dens, in his Theology, says of it: "It is a place in which the souls of the pious dead, obnoxious to temporal punishment, make satisfaction." The catechism of the Council of Trent gives this rather evasive view of it: "In the fire of purgatory the souls of just men are cleansed by a temporal punishment, in order to be admitted into their eternal country, into which nothing defiled entereth." The Douay Catechism gives the following short exposition of it:

"*Q.* Whither go such as die in mortal sin?
A. To Hell, to all eternity.

"*Q.* Whither go such as die in venial sin, or

not having fully satisfied for the punishment due to their mortal sins. *A.* To purgatory, till they have made full satisfaction for them, and then to Heaven."

Now what foundation has this division of sins into mortal and venial sins, this idea of making satisfaction for sin by suffering in the world to come, in the word of God? Simply none whatever. Still, the very Devil himself can quote Scripture, and we do not wonder, when we learn that Romanists make a faint show of defending their favorite doctrine from the Bible. It is but natural that they should. Protestant teaching has inspired so much love and reverence for the Bible, that they must for the sake of public opinion, make some show of proving their doctrines by it. Even tradition and the fathers are not quite enough. So they give us a few passages of Scripture. They refer to 1 Cor. iii., 13, 14, 15. "Every man's work shall be made manifest, for the day shall declare it, because it shall be revealed by fire: and the fire shall try every man's work, of what sort it is. If any man's work abide which he hath built thereon, he shall receive a reward. If any man's work shall be burned, he shall suffer loss: but he himself shall be saved, yet so as by fire."

This fire, however, is not as the fire of purgatory is supposed to be, to purify men's souls, but to try *every man's work*. *Every man's work* is to be tried: but purgatory is only gotten up for the benefit of good Roman Catholics. Poor Protestants have no such chance of salvation after death. It does not say that persons are saved by fire, but only, so *as by fire*—that is, with great difficulty. By carefully reading the text and context, any one may understand this beautiful passage of Scripture. "A good man, who, on the precious foundation of Jesus Christ, builds worthless materials, such as wood, hay, stubble, shall suffer the loss of his works, yet he himself shall be saved, though with great difficulty, *so as by fire.*"—*Nevins on Popery, page* 155.

Matt. v., 25, 26, is urged in favor of purgatory: "Agree with thine adversary quickly, whilst thou art in the way with him; lest at any time the adversary deliver thee to the judge, and the judge deliver thee to the officer, and thou be cast into prison. Verily, I say unto thee, thou shalt by no means come out thence till thou hast paid the uttermost farthing."

This text has about as much to do with purgatory as the man in the moon. To present a clear exposition of it is the very best way to refute the false doctrine that has been founded upon it. This I will do by quoting from Whedon's invaluable commentary: "The whole is a symbolical representation of divine judgment, as is shown by the next verse, in which justice without mercy is inflexibly declared. The *Adversary* stands for our offended God. *Quickly* and *the way* stand for the brief period of our probation. The *Judge* is the Son of Man at his coming. *The officer* is the judicial angel. Matt. xxv., 31. The *prison* is *Hell*. Sentiment: repair every wrong before divine justice inflict punishment to the utmost." Is not this exposition clear, simple, beautiful? To what straits must men be reduced when they press this text into the service of purgatory? The words of Christ concerning the sin against the Holy Ghost, are sometimes pressed into this controversy by Romanists. "The blasphemy against the Holy Ghost shall not be forgiven, neither in this world nor the world to come."—Matt. xii., 32. Does not this, they inquire, imply that there will be forgiveness in the world to come? It implies no such thing. This form of expression is simply used to strengthen the affirmation. If any one doubts this, let him just look at the parallel passages in Mark and Luke.

Mark says, that the blasphemy *hath never forgiveness*, and Luke, that this blasphemy *shall not be forgiven him.*—Mark iii., 29; Luke xii., 10.

Sometimes we are told with a great flourish of triumph, that Christ went and preached to the spirits in prison, and does not, they ask, this settle the question? The reader is referred to 1 Peter, iii., 18, 19, 20. He will there find, first, that this preaching took place "in the day of Noah, while the ark was a preparing." Second, that it was "by the Spirit," that Christ preached.

Third, that the persons to whom this preaching was sent, was the antediluvians. Fourth, that the prison was the earth on which they then lived. So clear is it, that this text gives no support to the doctrine of purgatory, that a number of Roman Catholic writers have themselves given it up. We have now examined the texts of Scripture put forth in favor of this horrid doctrine. Let us look for a moment at the clear Scripture testimony against it. I hardly know where to begin, so numerous are the declarations of Scripture that bear against the existence of a purgatory for departed spirits. Remember, that this purgatory is for God's children. The blood of Christ is not enough. Sin must be burnt out in fire, not washed away in Jesus' blood. Paul said: "I am in a strait betwixt two, having a desire *to depart* and be with Christ, which is better."—Phil. i., 23. This does not look much as though he expected to stop in purgatory.

"We know that if our earthly house of this tabernacle were dissolved, we have a building of God, a house not made with hands, eternal in the heavens." — 2 Cor. v., 1. Somehow this passage does not look much in the direction of purgatory. In another place we are told that to be "absent from the body" is to be "present with the Lord." *Is the Lord in purgatory?* A voice from heaven declares that the dead in the Lord are blessed, and that they "rest from their labours." What kind of rest could a person obtain if racked by the pains of purgatory? This inquiry might be continued much longer, but enough has been presented to show that the Romish fiction of purgatory has no foundation in Scripture. Prayers for the dead grow out of the doctrine of purgatory. This is one of the ways by which the unhappy souls escape. If they are poor, and have no rich friends to pay for masses and prayers, they must remain in purgatory until they suffer enough to atone for their sins. But if they have rich friends to see that masses are said "for the repose of their souls," their departure may be hastened. The priests seem to know all about the state of departed souls. Else why do they say masses for the repose of a departed soul for a season, and then give the matter up? If the soul is not in purgatory, these prayers are useless, and had better be offered in behalf of some one else. And why do they cease saying masses, unless they *know* that the soul is liberated? To do this would be cruel. Yet masses are not said forever for the repose of a soul. Some only have a mass said at the funeral. Others, again, keep it up for several months, or a year. All this seems strange. Surely, the priests must know when to stop, when the soul is liberated. But, then, *how do they know?* Would it not be awful if they stopped too soon, and left the soul in torment? Another curious thing about these prayers for the dead is, that they wait so long, sometimes. They do not keep right at it, until the work is done. Sometimes months, and even years, intervene between the masses.

It may be very nice for friends on earth to have things done in this quiet, genteel way; but how about the poor soul in purgatory? I think that I should want them to hurry up.

A very queer thing about these masses for the dead is, that they are very often *sung*. They *sing* for the repose of souls in purgatory. Is not that cruel? If you were burning in the fires of purgatory, would you think it kind in your friends on earth to get together and sing over it? Singing expresses joy and mirth. I will mention another strange feature in connection with these masses. When a Bishop or a Pope dies, they say more masses than they do for a common sinner,. and keep it up longer. Now, either the priests, bishops and popes are worse than the common run of men, or else the Church does not care so much for the souls of the poor and unknown. I do not care which horn of the dilemma they select. Now, when we put all these queer things together, does it not look as though they (I mean the clergy,) do not believe it themselves? How can they pass each other in the street and not *laugh*? But it is sad to think of the deluded flock. How dark the view that rises up before the dying papist! Nothing but fire and pain. The crown and harp are a great way off, and to reach them he must wade through smoke and flame. No wonder that we never hear of a Roman Catholic dying *shouting happy!* Death for him has a fearful sting, and the grave is robed in blackness. How different when a Christian dies. His lips may be wet with the dew of the vale, and his cold cheeks kissed by the spray of Jordan; yet all is well. Jesus waits to receive him, and the hosts of glory encamp about his dying pillow.

> "Sure the last end
> Of the good man is peace. How calm his exit!
> Night dews fall not more calmly on the ground,
> Nor weary, worn-out winds expire so soft."

It has often been my privilege to stand by the bed-side of departing saints, and witness the calmness and peace with which they looked forward to the life beyond.

O! Rome thou hast shut out the light of Bethlehem's star, and replaced the skeleton crown on Death's dark brow. We may almost say of thee, as the legends of the Rabbi say of Cain, that the flowers wither at thy touch, and the earth turns black beneath thy tread. The difference between thy teaching and the teaching of the Bible is best shown in the hour of death. I hope the reader will trust to Christ, and not to Rome. The *priest* may stand at your dying bed, with hallowed oil, holy water, crucifix and beads; yet these will give your soul no peace and comfort. But *Jesus* will make your death a transition to joys unknown.

Well has the poet said:

> "Oh! change — oh, wondrous change!
> Burst are the prison bars;
> This moment *there*, so low,
> So angonized, and now
> Beyond the stars.

> "O! change — stupendous change!
> There lies the soulless clod,
> The sun eternal breaks —
> The new immortal wakes —
> Wakes with his God."

CHAPTER X.

TO WHOM SHALL WE PRAY?

"*Let your requests be made known unto God.*"—Phil. iv., 6.

"Prayer is the Christian's vital breath,
The Christian's native air:
His watchword at the gates of death,—
He enters Heaven by prayer."
Montgomery.

PRAYER is the great duty of the Christian life. No man can lead a pious life without praying, any more than he could sustain physical life without eating. Prayer is the first indication of the new life, the first act of the awakened soul: while the last words of the expiring saint are often breathed in prayer. Prayer is a golden thread, woven by the shuttle of faith, all through the warp and woof of the Christian life. The question then, "to whom shall we pray?" is one of great importance. A mistake here may be fatal. Still, the question is soon answered by Protestants. We reply at once, to God and to God only. Now, we do not deny that Roman Catholics pray to God, but we do affirm that they do not pray to him alone. They pray to saints and angels, and to the Virgin Mary. They deny that they pray directly to the saints, and say that they simply ask the saints to pray for them, in the same manner that we request a like favor of earthly friends. This is all very well as a way to answer the inquiries of Protestants: but is it the truth? We think not: and shall present full proof of our charge. Roman Catholics *do* pray directly to the Virgin Mary and the saints, as directly as we pray to God. *They worship them.* Pope Gregory XVI., in his encyclical letter, addressed to all patriarchs, primates, archbishops, and bishops, dated August 15th, 1832, says: "We select for the date of our letter this most joyful day, on which we celebrate the solemn festival of the most blessed virgin's triumphant assumption into Heaven, that she who has been, through every great calamity, our patroness and protectress, may watch over us writing to you, and lead our mind, by her heavenly influence, to those counsels which may prove most salutary to Christ's flock."

Toward the conclusion of the same letter, he says: "But that all may have a successful and happy issue, let us raise our eyes to the most blessed Virgin Mary, who alone destroys heresies, who is our greatest hope, yea, the entire ground of our hope."

This is high praise to bestow on a creature. She (the Virgin Mary) is our only hope, its "entire ground." What room is left for Jesus, whom Protestants, who have no infallible pope to guide them, are wont to regard as the great foundation of all their hopes? We will now give the "Litany of the Blessed Virgin," a rigmarole of nonsense and blasphemy, to be found in nearly all Romish books of devotion:

"THE LITANY OF THE BLESSED VIRGIN."

"We fly to thy patronage, O holy mother of God! Despise not our petitions in our necessities, but deliver us from all dangers, O ever glorious and blessed virgin!

Lord! have mercy on us.
Christ! have mercy on us.
Lord! have mercy on us.
Christ! hear us. Christ! graciously hear us.
God the Father of Heaven, *have mercy on us.*
God the Son, Redeemer of the world, *have mercy on us.*
Holy Trinity, one God, *have mercy on us.*

  Holy Mary,
  Holy mother of God,
  Holy virgin of virgins,
  Mother of Christ,
  Mother of divine grace,
  Mother most pure,
  Mother most chaste,
  Mother undefiled,
  Mother unviolated,
  Mother most amiable,
  Mother most admirable,
  Mother of our Creator,
  Mother of our Redeemer,

PRAY FOR US.

Virgin most prudent,
Virgin most venerable,
Virgin most powerful,
Virgin most renowned,
Virgin most merciful,
Mother most faithful,
Mirror of justice,
Seat of wisdom,
Cause of our joy,
Spiritual vessel,
Vessel of honour,
Vessel of singular devotion,
Mystical rose,
Tower of ivory,
House of gold,
Ark of the covenant,
Gate of Heaven,
Morning star,
Health of the weak,
Refuge of sinners,
Comforter of the afflicted,
Help of Christians,
Queen of angels,

Pray for us.

Queen of patriarchs,
Queen of prophets,
Queen of apostles,
Queen of martyrs,
Queen of confessors,
Queen of virgins,
Queen of all saints,

PRAY FOR US.

Lamb of God! who takest away the sins of the world, spare us, Lord!

Lamb of God! who takest away the sins of the world, hear us.

Lord! have mercy on us.

Christ! hear us. Christ! graciously hear us.

Lord! have mercy on us! Christ! have mercy on us.

V. Pray for us, O holy mother of God.

B. That we may be worthy of the promises of Christ."

In this litany, some prayers, we admit, are directed to the Father and the Son, but the most of it is directly addressed to Mary. She is the "Gate of Heaven;" whereas Christ proclaims that He is the only way of entrance, the one great door.

She is the Morning Star, not Christ, as we read in Revelations. "I am the bright and morning star."— Rev. xxii., 16. She is the "Health of the weak," not Christ, the Great Physician. She is the "Refuge of sinners," the "Comforter of the afflicted," the "Help of Christians." Is not this gross idolatry, pure *creature worship?*

It is true they use the form, "Pray for us;" but, then, they mean, be our advocate, intercede for us; and they do this because of her supposed merits. When we ask for the prayers of our living friends, we make no mention of advocacy or merits. We think, after all, that it is most effectual, when we pray for ourselves. So their plea will not hold good. They cannot exonerate themselves from the charge of idolatry. They degrade the Lord Jesus by introducing a new mediator and intercessor. But the Bible declares that, "There is one God, and *one* mediator be-

tween God and men, the man Christ Jesus."—
1 Tim. ii., 8.

But they are not content with appealing to the Virgin Mary. They want any quantity of "strings to their bow." If one saint is well, a hundred saints are better. So they have a "Litany of Saints."

A whole string of saints are invited to act as our mediators. There seems to be hardly any room for Christ whatever. Yet the Bible declares that he is the *only Mediator*. Is it not, then, gross and shameless idolatry, for those calling themselves Christians, thus to invoke the whole host of heaven? But they give the Virgin Mary the pre-eminence. To her they not only pray, but *sing*. Yes, they *sing* to her. Their temples resound with her songs of praise.

From the 334th page of the Roman Missal, I subjoin a specimen of this form of idolatry:

"O, holy mother of our God!
To thee for help we fly;
Despise not this our humble prayer,
But all our wants supply.

> O! glorious Virgin, ever blest,
>   Defend us from our foes;
> From threatening danger set us free,
>   And terminate our woes."

According to this hymn, the Virgin Mary is the source to which they fly for help. She supplies their wants, protects them from their enemies, and terminates their sorrows. I am glad that I am not a Roman Catholic. Here is another of their hymns to the Virgin:

"AVE MARIS STELLA."

> "Hail, thou resplendent star
>   Which shineth o'er the main;
> Blest mother of our God,
>   And ever Virgin Queen.
>
> Hail, happy gate of bliss,
>   Greeted by Gabriel's tongue;
> *Negotiate our peace,*
>   *And cancel Eve's wrong.*
>
> *Loosen the sinner's bonds,*
>   All evils drive away;
> Bring light unto the blind,
>   And for all graces pray.
>
> Exert the mother's care,
>   And us thy children own;
> To Him convey our prayer,
>   Who chose to be thy Son.

O! pure, O! spotless maid,
    Whose meekness all surpass'd
Our lusts and passions quell,
    And make us mild and chaste.

Preserve our lives unstained,
    And guard us in our way,
Until we come to thee,
    To joys that ne'er decay.

Praise to the Father be,
    With Christ, his only Son,
And to the Holy Ghost,
    Thrice blessed Three in One."

This hymn teaches that Mary is the Saviour of the world. She

" Negotiates our peace,
    And cancels Eve's wrong."

She loosens the bands of the sinner, and brings light to the darkened mind. She sanctifies the heart and guides to endless peace. We Protestants think of Heaven, as the place where Jesus reigns, but the Romanists think of it as the place where Mary reigns. We love to think of meeting with Jesus, they love to think of meeting with Mary. We think that Mary was a good woman, was highly honored in being the mother of Jesus, and is now in Heaven. But is that any reason why we should *worship* her? Is it any reason why we should pray to her, sing to her, dedicate churches to her, and adore her images and pictures? This creature worship, this adoration of Mary and the saints, runs all through their preaching, their prayer books, their newspapers. The worship of the creature has supplanted the worship of the Creator.

Let us see how this worship of, and praying to saints, looks in the light of Scripture. This is the great test. Before it the idolatry and superstition of Rome melt away like dew on the mountains. We have already seen that we are invited to make our wants known unto God, and that there can be only one mediator between him and us, " the man Christ Jesus." Prayer is most certainly one method of worship. Singing is another. Now, the Romanists pray and sing to Mary and the saints; hence they worship them. How this does agree with the solemn declaration, " Thou shalt worship the Lord thy God, and him only shalt thou serve."—Matt. iv., 10.

Here is another passage that ought to make Romanists tremble with fear and guilt: "Let no man beguile you of your reward in a voluntary humility and worshipping of angels, intruding into those things which he hath not seen, vainly puffed up by his fleshy mind."—Col. ii., 18.

Elijah did not seem to be acquainted with the Romish ways, for he said to Elisha, "Ask what I shall do for thee before I be taken away from thee."—2 Kings ii., 9.

If Elijah expected to be prayed to in a future state, what was the need of this admonition? Peter (Romanists regard him as their First Pope,) seems to have been a bit of a Protestant; for when Cornelius fell down at his feet, and worshipped him, Peter raised him up, and said: "Stand up; I myself am a man." This is not much after the manner of modern Popes.

Now, if we are not to worship saints when on the earth, why should we worship them when taken to Heaven? But we have a case in the Bible where the worship of a saint in Heaven was directly rebuked and forbidden. John, the beloved disciple, fell down to adorn the angel showing unto him the heavenly glory; but he said unto him, "*See thou do it not;* I am thy fellow-servant, and of thy brethren that have the testimony of Jesus; worship God."—Rev. xix., 10.

If all the angels and saints feel and act like this, one-half of the praying done in Roman Catholic Churches had much better be omitted. As for the worship of Mary, Christ treated her with kindness and respect, loved her as his mother, but has never indicated that she should be worshipped or prayed to, never announced her as the Queen of Heaven, or as a mediator between him and us. So far from this, he seems to have guarded his followers against excessive reverence for her.

"One said unto him, Behold thy mother and thy brethren stand without, desiring to speak with thee. But he answered and said unto them that told him, Who is my mother? and who are my brethren? And he stretched forth his hand towards his disciples, and said: Behold my mother and my brethren! For whosoever shall do the will of my Father, which is in heaven, the same is my brother, and sister, and mother."—Matt. xii., 47–50.

What a rebuke do we have here to the disgusting Idolatry of Romanism. But they still persist in telling us that the mother of Jesus never sinned as other mortals; that she never lived with Joseph as his wife; that she was taken up bodily to heaven; that she is queen of angels and saints; has supreme command over the heart of Jesus, and must be adored and prayed to.

The Church of Rome is the "Church of Mary," not the "Church of Jesus." The most prominent object in her hymns, her prayers, and in her teachings, is Mary. To Mary her altars are dedicated, and in honor of Mary her churches are built. It is throughout *Marianity*, rather than *Christianity*. Is it not strange that if the teaching of this Church is correct, we should read nothing about Mary in the epistles of the primitive apostles? Paul, James, and Peter, in their several letters, do not even mention her. John, in his visions of the heavenly world, saw the Lamb in the midst of the throne, but makes no mention of Mary, whom Romanists regard as heaven's great queen. This was certainly a very grave omission.

The reader may now see the great difference between Romanism and Protestantism on the subject of prayer. We have only the great and the glorious God to pray to, and feel that we need no other refuge. Romanists direct a great part of their praying to Mary, to the saints and angels. We only pray to God, because we have no Scriptural warrant for praying to any other Being. This ground has been already gone over. I will only add that we have one instance in the New Testament of praying to saints. The rich man prayed in hell, but his prayer was never answered. The Roman Catholics are welcome to get all the aid they can from this single case of praying to saints. We should hardly know how to pray to the saints, even if we wished to. If we should pray to them in a general way, it would be a random sort of work. We fear that we would not gain much by the operation, as it might be with them as it is with their brethren on earth, that "what is everybody's business, soon comes to be regarded as nobody's business." If we do not pray in this general manner, but select individual saints, we ought to know just who are in heaven and who are not. But this we do not know, nor will we know who are in heaven until we get there ourselves. God alone can look down into the human heart, and tell who are truly loving and serving him. Now, suppose we should make a mistake, and pray to some one not in heaven, of what avail would our prayers be? But waiving this difficulty, how are we to know that the saint to whom we pray hears us? The saints are not omnipresent. The distance between them and us is very great, and how do we know that a saint can hear a thousand prayers, addressed to him from a thousand parts of the earth at the same time? Besides all this, praying to saints is a very roundabout way of getting access to our heavenly Father. Why not go at once to God? He loves to have us come to him, invites and even urges us to come. In fact, we have a *standing invitation*.

Why not, then, improve it? For these and many other reasons we prefer to pray to God only. We love the saints and angels. We love to think of the time when we may fellowship with them, but we do not *pray* to them. We do not worship them. We never worshipped them when on the earth, and do not feel inclined to worship them now that they are in heaven. We have never felt any loss from this action.

We have always found God an all-sufficient Friend. We never expect to exhaust the fountain of Divine goodness. We have yet to learn that Romanists bear the ills of life, with more calmness or trust in God than Protestants. We will conclude this chapter with a brief refutation of the arguments commonly advanced by Roman Catholics in defence of their saint worship.

It has been said that we ought to worship the saints, because of their supernatural excellence. But mere excellence is no ground for adoration.

If it were, every inferior being should worship the rank of beings above him. There are many excellent persons on earth, but we do not feel that we ought to worship them. Dens rests the matter on the authority of the church, but we deny the authority of the church to establish a species of worship, which is not supported by the Word of God. He also says: "that the saints are to be invoked, because the Council of Trent has enjoined it." To this we still reply, that we regard nothing as an infallible guide in matters of faith and practice save the Word of God. It has been said that subjects cannot go directly to their king, but have to approach him through his ministers. To this queer argument, we reply that the illustration does not hold good. The doings of God are not to be judged by human proceedings. His ways are not as our ways, or his thoughts as our thoughts.

Earthly governments are weak and imperfect, but this is not the case with the Divine Government. They argue that Christ is too great to be touched by our miseries, too exalted to be approached by us, that the saints are more human, etc. This we flatly deny. The New Testament everywhere speaks of Jesus as tender and loving. He can "be touched with the feeling of our infirmities." A few more arguments might be mentioned, but as they are about like those already given, the reader will not require their examination. The Church of Rome stands charged with gross idolatry. She worships the creature more than she does the Creator. This is a mill-stone that will yet sink her beneath the waves of oblivion. May God hasten the time. Her dark shadow comes between the soul and God at every turn. She sends her children for aid and grace to nearly everything but God. May God in his own good time, reveal himself to them, and bring them out into the light.

CHAPTER XI.

CELIBACY.

"*Marriage is honorable in all.*"—HEB. xiii., 4.

"*A bishop, then, must be blameless, the husband of one wife.*"—1 TIM. iii., 2.

"*Let the deacons be the husbands of one wife, ruling their children and their own houses well.*"—1 TIM. iii., 12.

"Domestic happiness, thou only bliss
Of Paradise, that hast survived the fall."
Cowper.

THE love of one man for one woman, and the life-long union of such devoted hearts, in the holy estate of matrimony, is a most blessed and a divine institution. This benign ordinance escaped the wreck of Eden, and has been handed down to us. Even this pure and heaven-ordained institution, has not escaped the withering touch of Romanism. One would think that so fair a flower might have been allowed to bloom and flourish unharmed; but it has not been the case. Rome teaches that there is a holier, a more exalted state, than that of marriage. It is better, says Rome, to live in a single than in a married state. Surely, this looks like an improvement on the word of God. Man has become purer than his Maker. The tenth canon of the Council of Trent on the subject of marriage, reads as follows: "Whoever shall affirm that the conjugal state is to be preferred to a life of virginity or celibacy, and that it is not better and more conducive to happiness to remain in virginity, or celibacy, than to be married, let him be accursed."

Their catechism puts it in this form: "The words increase and multiply, which were uttered by Almighty God, do not impose on every individual an obligation to marry; they declare the object of the institution of marriage; and now that the human race is widely diffused, not only is there no law rendering marriage obligatory, but, on the contrary, virginity is highly exalted and strongly recommended in Scripture, as superior to marriage, as a state of greater perfection and holiness."

This is certainly a strange doctrine. We admit that no one is obligated to marry, that it is no sin to remain in an unmarried state; but that celibacy is holier and more pleasing to God than a married life, does seem strange, indeed. Perhaps it is because we have read the Bible so much. The Bible can be very well understood without Romanism, and Romanism can certainly get along without the Bible; but to receive both, and then try to reconcile them, is a most puzzling task.

God himself instituted marriage. He joined our first parents together in this holy state, and bade them, "Be fruitful, and multiply, and replenish the earth."

Paul, writing to the Church at Corinth on the subject of marriage, says: "Nevertheless, to avoid fornication, let every man have his own wife, and let every woman have her own husband." In writing to his son in the gospel, Timothy, the same apostle says: "I will, therefore, that the younger women marry, bear children, guide the house, give none occasion to the adversary to speak reproachfully." It is declared honorable in all; and is especially enjoined on those who take holy orders.

The first miracle of Christ was performed at a wedding; and from the relations of husband and wife are drawn many tender and beautiful illustrations, setting forth the union between Christ and his people.

The more I see of Romish folly, and the more I contrast its teachings with the Bible, the less do I wonder that they dislike so much to see this blessed book circulated and read. What would Roman Catholics think, if taking up the Bible, they should read that marriage is "Honorable in all," or that a bishop "must be the husband of one wife"? If the Church of Rome wishes to retain its hold upon the people, it had better continue its old plan of keeping the Bible away from them. We give them credit for seeing and carefully guarding their weak point. For the sake, however, of us Bible-loving Protestants, and that great regard for the Bible which pervades the entire community, they do make a faint show of defending their doctrine from the Bible. They well know that in order to make converts from the ranks of Protestantism, they must pretend to have some little regard for the Bible. For their own people they have a much more direct and pleasing method. The voice of the Infallible Church is enough for them.

Well, for the sake of us Protestants, they try to defend their horrid doctrine of celibacy from the Bible. It is a sorry sort of defence, but none of us would be likely to do any better, if we had so poor a cause and so little to sustain it. They appeal to the first epistle of Paul to the Corinthians, the seventh chapter. We admit that in this chapter there are some expressions that seem to favor a single state. But the explanation is very easy. The Church was soon to undergo a terrible persecution; even then to be a Christian brought reproach and peril. In such a state of things common prudence would suggest great caution in entering upon the married state. As we have before said, no man is obligated to marry, and it may often be a question of great moment, whether it be best to enter upon married life, or to remain single. Such was the state of things in the minds of many, when Paul wrote to the Church at Corinth. The key to the whole chapter is given in the 26th verse: "I suppose this is good for the present distress." Yet, even under these circumstances, he does not command any man, or class of men, to abstain from marriage, but expressly declares that it is lawful for all. So much for the argument drawn from the seventh chapter of Corinthians.

Sometimes Matt. xix., 12, is quoted in favor of Romish celibacy. We read in this verse, that " There be eunuchs, which have made themselves eunuchs for the Kingdom of Heaven's sake." These, however, are rare and special cases. It may sometimes happen that men are called to some work that they can perform better if free from the care of a family.

The reader will recall the case of Bishop Asbury and the early American Methodist preachers, as furnishing a good illustration of the fact just stated. In those days of severe toil and great poverty, it were well nigh impossible for preachers to provide for and watch over the interests of a wife and family.

The celibacy referred to by Christ, and of which the early Methodist preachers in this country form an example, is only for those able to receive and practice it. After all, it is only *permitted*, not *commanded*. The celibacy in the Church of Rome is forced, and often leads to fearful sin and shameless lust. The following passage is perhaps more frequently cited in favor of celibacy than any other: "The children of this world marry, and are given in marriage; but they which are worthy to obtain that world and the resurrection from the dead, neither marry nor are given in marriage; neither can they die any more; for they are equal unto the angels; and are the children of God, being the children of the resurrection." — Luke xx., 34-36.

"The plain meaning of this passage is, that marriage is the condition of our present mode of existence; but it is not the condition of the future life. According to the Roman Catholic interpretation of this passage we might argue, 'Animal life is sustained by aliment; not so the angelic life; therefore to abstain from food, as far as possible, is in the same degree to make one's self an angel.' " — *Elliott on Romanism, Vol. II., page* 385.

We will not pursue this investigation into the Bible argument in behalf of celibacy any farther. One or two more passages might be given, as sometimes quoted by Romanists; but before they can by any means be pressed into the service of Romanism, they must receive so fanciful an interpretation, and be so grossly perverted, that to formally consider them, and refute the meaning forced upon them, would be an insult to the intelligence of the reader. We object, then, to the Popish doctrine of celibacy, that it has no support or foundation in Scripture. We object also that it is absurd. All men ought to be as holy as they can. If celibacy is a holier state than matrimony, no man ought to be married. Well, suppose we all practice celibacy. There would soon be none left to argue concerning which is the better way: unless we adopted the practice of Rome, and allowed fornication, because too pure to enter upon matrimony. This may seem a severe charge, but we appeal to well-known facts. If Father Walsh, the would-be seducer of Miss Edith O'Gorman, had taken to himself a wife, he would soon have been hurried out of the church and ministry: but as he only attempted to ruin a poor and defenceless nun, he is now and always has been an ordained priest in the Romish Church.

All the punishment he received was a removal from one parish to another. I think I can understand why the Church of Rome forbids its priests to marry. If they marry, and rear families, they will form social and political ties. They will cease to be the mere tools of the Pope. They will contract a love of country, and the great binding power of the Papacy will be broken. As it is now, they can easily be transferred from one country to another, or employed to great advantage as spies and politicians. This gives the Pope an immense power.

We object to celibacy as maintained and practiced in the Roman Catholic Church, that it produces a fearful amount of licentiousness. It has done this in the past, and it is doing it to-day. A tree is known by its fruits. If celibacy is such a holy state, it ought to fill the earth with blessing. The voice of history tells a very different story.

In the third century Cyprian complains bitterly of the conduct of the celibates of his day. He tells us that males and females occupy the same bed, although living under a vow of celibacy. In the fourth century, Chrysostom admits of conduct in the professed virgins of his day, as gross as that described by Cyprian.

Udalric, bishop of Augusta, who flourished several centuries later, tells us: " That Gregory the Great, by his decree, deprived priests of their wives; when, shortly after, he commanded that some fish should be caught from the fish-ponds, the fishers, instead of fish, found the heads of six thousand infants that had been drowned in the pond." These, he tells us, " were born from the concealed fornications and adulteries of the priests." Bernard, who died in 963, speaking of the celibates of his day, says: "Nay, besides fornications, adulteries, and incests, there are not wanting among some the most shameful and ignominious conduct."

Thus we might go through each successive century, and show by competent witnesses, how degraded and vile have been the lives of the great majority of those professing celibacy. In our days, we have no reason to believe that things are much improved. Those professing celibacy are simply men and women, with all the passions and infirmities of our frail humanity. They are, in general, *unconverted* men and women. They live high, on rich foods and wines. They have free access to each other's society. They can easily conceal their guilt. For these and other reasons, we believe that Romish celibacy is still a fearful curse, and a fruitful source of crime.

CHAPTER XII.

THE CONVENT SYSTEM.

"*God hath made man upright; but they have sought out many inventions.*"—Eec. vii., 29.

AS the Church of Rome ascribes great merit to a life of celibacy, so likewise she ascribes great merit to a life of solitude. The great doctrinal error at the foundation of these false views of human life is, that the atonement of Christ is not in itself sufficient to save the soul. It must be supplemented by penance and self-inflicted pain in this life, and the fires of purgatory in the life to come. Protestants believe that the followers of Christ must often bear the cross of suffering and painful toil in this life; but they do not believe that Christians should seek for suffering, or that they should inflict it upon themselves. Neither do they regard Christian suffering and toil as vicarious, or in any way as adding to the perfect work of Christ. Romanists seem to think that the more miserable we are in this world, the happier we will be in the next. They think that human suffering may become vicarious, and transfer merit to others, by making the soul of the sufferer advance in sacrifice and purity beyond the requirements of the law of God.

This surplus of holiness and good works, constitute what they are pleased to call the "Celestial Treasury of Indulgences," and is generously retailed by the Holy Father in prices to suit the pockets of the various purchasers. We can now very easily understand the rise of the convent system. We see the nature of the foundation on which it rests.

The heart of man is given to pride. The Bible plan of salvation does not flatter this proud heart—sin must be confessed and forsaken, eternal life must be received as the free and unmerited gift of God. All this is very repulsive to the proud and unrenewed heart. Man would *earn* salvation. He would *buy* it. He would rather get it in any way, than as a free and unmerited *gift*. Very early in the history of the Christian Church, did this self-righteous spirit begin to manifest itself. Even in the life-time of Paul, the Mystery of Iniquity began to work. Once having commenced, this vile cancer of monkery continued to spread, until it threatened to eat away the last remaining semblance of Christianity. Says Dr. Ruter, in his "Church History," speaking of the fourth century: " Another branch of superstition, which daily increased, was Monkery; the actual establishment of which is to be dated from the fourth century. Numbers, seized by a fanatical spirit, voluntarily inflicted upon themselves the severest sufferings, and were content to be deprived of every earthly good. In this solitary state, like their leader, the illiterate Anthony, they rejected learning as useless, if not pernicious, and professed to be occupied solely in silence, meditation and prayer. When, however, they were formed into regular societies, they employed some part of their time in study. Their melancholy modes of life prepared and qualified them for all the vagaries of a heated imagination; they had prophetic dreams, saw visions, conversed with the different inhabitants of the invisible world, and many closed a life of despair in madness. Considerable numbers of the softer sex forsook their elegant abodes, and all the endearments of domestic life, to dwell in caves and deserts. Egypt was the great theater for monastic action; and at the close of the fourth century, it was computed that twenty-seven thousand monks and nuns were to be found in that country. The fortunate Anthony had the happiness, in traversing the deserts, to discover the retreat of Paul, the hermit, whose eyes he piously closed, and resolved to imitate his holy example. His solitude was soon enlivened by numbers, for whose government he composed regulations, which were in a short time introduced, by his disciple Hilarion, into Syria and Palestine, and by others into Mesopotamia and Armenia. From the East it passed with celerity into the West. Basil introduced it into Greece, and Ambrose into Italy. Martin, the celebrated bishop of

Tours, propagated monkery so rapidly in Gaul, that his funeral is said to have been attended by no less than two thousand monks. The numbers of these deluded people, and the veneration paid to them were such as to induce them sometimes to conceive themselves superior to the laws, the execution of which they frequently suspended, and ventured with impunity to snatch criminals from the hands of justice while on their way to execution."—*Church History, pages* 75, 76.

In the next century matters grew still worse. Of monkery in this century, Dr. Ruter says: "The approbation of monastic institutions was not only extensively diffused, and numbers made unhappy from the defection of their relations, and the consequent loss of their support, but the more judicious part of the community had the mortification to observe that, as the numbers who embraced the state of monachism sensibly increased, so also monastic folly increased in the same proportion. In the beginning of this century a new order of monks was instituted by a person of the name of Alexander, who obtained the name of watchers, from their method of performing divine service without any intermission. They divided themselves into three classes, which relieved each other at stated hours; and by that means continued, without any interval, a perpetual course of divine service. Among the Mystics, many not only affected to reside with wild and savage beasts, but imitated their manners. With a ferocious aspect they traversed the gloomy deserts, fed upon herbs and grass, or remained motionless in certain places for several years, exposed to the scorching heat of the mid-day sun, or to the chilling blast of the nocturnal air. All conversation with men was studiously avoided by these gloomy fanatics, who frequently concluded their lives by an act of violent madness, or shut themselves up in narrow and miserable dens, to howl out the remainder of their wretched existence."—*Church History, page* 101.

It would be an easy task to follow out the development of this miserable superstition during the succeeding centuries. It still exists in the Church of Rome. Men and women still think that they can please God, and secure a high place in Heaven, by shutting themselves up from the busy world, and spending their years in undisturbed seclusion. Two things, however, are overlooked.

First, They do not escape temptation by rushing into the cloister of some convent. They take with them our frail and imperfect human nature. The human heart is the same in convent and in hall. The devil, our soul's arch enemy, cannot be shut out by gates and bars.

Secondly, They lose noble opportunities for doing good. Some nuns, we know, lead busy lives among the sick and suffering; but others are called cloistered nuns, and never leave the convent, even for the purpose of public worship.

Now, what right has any one, professing to be a follower of Jesus, to shut himself up in useless and inglorious solitude? Admitting that even cloistered nuns, do not lead lives of utter uselessness, how much more good might be accomplished if freed from the vows and fetters of convent life!

Think of the sorrowing hearts to be comforted, of the hungry to be fed, the sick and dying to be visited, the sinful to be directed to the cross. What would Paul and Peter, Dorcas or Phebe, have done for the Church and the world, if they had been monks and nuns in some gloomy convent?

But in their day convents were unknown. Christ never founded any, Peter never saw one. The whole tenor of the Bible is opposed to this dark system. We are to "Let our light shine;" to be as "A city that is set on a hill." I wonder if any Romish bishop, when preaching a sermon on the occasion of some impulsive girl taking the black veil, ever selected for his text, Matt. v., 15: "Neither do men light a candle, and put it under a bushel, but on a candlestick; and it giveth light unto all that are in the house." I should very much love to hear a sermon preached from such a text, on such an occasion. The convent system, like celibacy, is not only unscriptural, but absurd. If it is such a grand institution, all ought to have the advantage of it.

All Christians want to be as holy as it is possible for them to be. Well, suppose we all go into convents, and become monks and nuns, what is to become of a world perishing in sin?

The convent system is cruel. It tramples on the purest and best instincts of the human heart. It takes young and impulsive creatures, fills their minds with glowing conceptions of the purity and bliss of convent life, binds them by the most awful of vows, to a loveless and dreary life.

The false step has been taken. Soon the bright dreams are dispelled. Sleeping on comfortless beds in narrow cells, getting up at four o'clock in mid-winter, and a complete severance from all human loves; with ghostly fathers, priestly brothers, jealous sisters, and a snappish old superior for mother, is found to be anything but romantic and pleasing. Repentance comes too late. The fatal vow has been taken, and death alone can bring relief.

Thackeray, in his *Irish Sketch Book*, has said some truthful words. Would that all thinking to enter upon convent life, might read and ponder them. Referring to the Ursuline convents at Black Rock, near Cork, he says: "In the grille is a little wicket, and a ledge before it. It is to this wicket that women are brought to kneel; and a bishop is in a chapel on the other side, and takes their hands in his, and receives their vows. I had never seen the like before, and felt a sort of shudder in looking at the place. There rests the girl's knees as she offers herself up, and forswears the sacred affections which God gave her; there she kneels and denies forever the beautiful duties of her being—no tender maternal yearnings — no gentle attachments are to be had from her or for her — there she kneels and commits suicide upon her heart. O, honest Martin Luther! thank God you came to pull that infernal, wicked, unnatural altar down—that cursed Paganism. I came out of the place quite sick; and looking before me, there, thank God! was the blue spire of Minkstown church, soaring up into the free sky — a river in front rolling away to the sea — liberty, sunshine, all sorts of gladness and motion, roundabout; and I couldn't but thank Heaven for it, and the Being whose service is freedom, and who has given us affections that we may use them — not smother and kill them; and a noble world to live in, that we may admire it and Him who made it — not shrink from it, as though we dared not live there, but must turn our back upon *it* and its bountiful Provider. I declare, I think, for my part, that we have as much right to permit Sutterism in India as to allow women in the United Kingdom to take these wicked vows, or Catholic bishops to receive them."

These convents, it must be remembered, are shut out from public inspection. No one can enter them, or have any interview with any of their inmates, unless allowed so to do by the Romish authorities in charge.

A few years ago a motion was made in the British Parliament, and carried by a small majority, to appoint a committee to inquire into conventual and monastic institutions. In referring to the agitation growing out of the question, the *London Watchman* justly made the following remarks:

"The convents are prisons. They are built, as every one may see, almost strongly enough to stand a seige. High walls, massive doors, formidable fastenings, grates and bars of portentious solidity — are these things the favored instruments of liberty? Or are they the habitual weapons of tyranny and oppression? The convents *are* prisons; at least, ' the show of their countenance doth witness against them.' Women enter them under compulsion; remain in them under severe and terrible restraint; and disappear from them entirely, leaving no trace behind. It is well known that convents in this country are in communication with convents abroad, and that refractory nuns, or young women who have not yet taken the conventual vows, and about whom unpleasant inquiries are made by friends or lovers, are removed to the Continent; out of reach, sometimes forever out of reach, of all whom they love. As if to give special point to Mr. Newdegate's arguments, only a few days before he raised this question in the House, an unsuccessful attempt was made to remove a young woman to some convent-prison in France. Happily, the pursuit of her friends and her own vigorous resistance baffled the attempt; but no one who heard her cries for help resounding through the hotel where her spiritual guardians detained her for the night, could well believe that this 'bride of heaven' *voluntarily* 'sought the refuge of the cloister.'"

In this country, they are no better. We sincerely hope the time will come when these institutions will be annually inspected by officers appointed expressly for this purpose. We inspect prisons and lunatic asylums, why not inspect convents? God only knows how many, like Mary Ann Smith, have been abducted and confined in them: or how many would fain be restored to society and liberty if they only had the opportunity. If these words of warning shall lead any to turn aside from the snare, ere they take the fatal and unnatural vows upon them, or shall in any way hasten the time when these prisons shall be inspected by proper officers, the author will be amply repaid for all his toil.

CHAPTER XIII.

MINOR FOLLIES.

"The Mother of Harlots and Abominations of the Earth."—
REV. xvii., 5.

IN comparing the doctrines and doings of Romanism, with the teaching of Holy Writ, we cannot fail to perceive a wide departure from Scriptural simplicity. We have gone over much of this ground, but have not yet completed the list of Papal abominations. Wishing to make this book rather a brief manual on the subject of Romanism, than an extended and exhaustive treatise; and having yet to consider the position of Rome in prophecy, its cruel and bloodthirsty persecutions, the danger with which it threatens our national life, together with its certain and utter overthrow, we will compress our examination of some remaining Romish abominations into the space of a single chapter. Of course a mere outline can only be given. We hope that many of our readers will be led to make a thorough comparison of Romish doings, with the pure and infallible word of God: Those who do this, will never follow in the footsteps of Doane, Rogers or Dr. Stone; unless their desire of notoriety and gain is greater than their love for truth. If you should go to worship in some Roman Catholic Church, you would find it a very different affair from a Presbyterian, Baptist, Methodist, or any other truly Protestant Church. Perhaps the first thing to attract your attention, would be a little vessel filled with water, (often not over-clean) and fastened to the wall in the vestibule. This is the far-famed *holy water*. A little salt and a few other ingredients are put in some common water, a blessing is added by the priest or bishop, and behold! we have "holy water." This holy water is put to many different uses, and is supposed to possess untold merits. It is supposed to keep away the Devil, prevent sickness and to ward off harm of every possible kind. The people dip their fingers in it, and then cross themselves. They sometimes carry it away in little bottles, and sprinkle it on their beds, in order to keep away the Devil, and to prevent danger and accident.

"One of the most senseless and extraordinary uses to which the papists apply this holy water, is the sprinkling and blessing of *horses*, mules, *asses*, &c., on the festival of St. Anthony, observed annually on the 17th of January. On that day the inhabitants of the city of Rome and vicinity send their horses, &c., decked with ribbons, to the convent of St. Anthony, which is situated near the Church of St. Mary the Great.

"The priest, in his sacerdotal garments, stands at the church door, with a large sprinkling-brush in his hand, and as each animal is presented to him, he takes off his skull cap, mutters a few words in Latin, intimating that through the merits of the blessed St. Anthony, they are to be preserved for the coming year from sickness and death, famine and danger, then dips his brush in a huge bucket of holy water, that stands by him, and sprinkles them in the name of the Father, and of the Son, and of the Holy Ghost. Sometimes the visitor at Rome will see a splendid equipage driven up, attended by outriders, in elegant livery, to have the horses thus sprinkled with holy water, all the people remaining uncovered till the absurd and disgusting ceremony is over. On one occasion a traveler observed a countryman, whose beast having received the holy water, set off from the church door at a galop, but had scarcely gone a hundred yards before the ungainly animal tumbled down with him, and over its head he rolled into the dust. He soon, however, rose, and so did the horse, without either seeming to have sustained much injury. The priest looked on, and though his blessing had failed, he was not out of countenance; while some of the bystanders said that but for it, the horse and its rider might have broken their necks."—*Dowling's History of Romanism, pages* 117–118.

Now, what warrant in the Bible can we find for such degrading ceremonies, such absurd superstition? It is not enough to say that the Bible does not condemn it. We should have some positive foundation, on which to rest it. Many things are not forbidden in the Bible, simply because when the Bible was composed, these modern follies were unknown. But it does not seem to fit in with the general spirit of the Bible. When the Bible is silent upon a point on which we seek information, we test the matter by an appeal to its general spirit and tone. Now, the general tone of the Bible is opposed to such operations. Holy water was unknown to the Jewish priest, unknown to Christ and to his apostles. We can trace the origin of this superstition to no very flattering source. It is manifestly transmitted from Paganism. Roman Catholic writers themselves have been compelled to admit this. This matter of holy water may be deemed by some as a thing of small importance; but it serves to illustrate the corruptions and follies of Romanism. Passing now within the church, we find it filled with images and pictures of Mary and the saints. To these the people kneel, and before them, at least, they engage in prayer. This certainly has a very heathenish and idolatrous appearance. We can hardly get away from the impression that we are in some heathen temple. Romanists tell us that their people only pray *before* them, and not *to* them: that the worship given them is only of a relative and secondary kind, &c.; but after all it *looks* at least very much like idolatry, and we have been warned to avoid even the "appearance of evil." Let us put the language of the Council of Trent, and that of the Word of God, side by side, that we may compare them. This is the language of the Council: "I most firmly assert, that the images of Christ, of the mother of God, ever virgin, and also of the saints, ought to be had and retained, and that due honor and veneration is to be given them." This is the language of the Word of God: "Thou shalt not make unto thee any graven image, or any likeness of any thing that is in heaven above, or that is in the earth beneath, or that is in the water under the earth: Thou shalt not bow down thyself to them, nor serve them."

I leave the reader to decide the question, whether the Council and the Bible entirely agree. The practice of the Romish Church is even worse than its doctrine on this subject. The ignorant at least *do pray* to them and *do worship* them. In Rome they have actually taken old heathen gods, given them Christian names, and set them up for the adoration of the people.

"The noblest heathen temple now remaining in the world, is the Pantheon, or Rotunda; which, as the inscription over the portico informs us, having been impiously dedicated of old by Agrippa to Jove, and all the gods, was impiously reconsecrated by Pope Boniface IV., about A. D. 610, To The Blessed Virgin And All The Saints.

Pantheon, &c.

Ab Agrippa Augusti Genero,

Impie Jovi Cæterisq; Mendocibus Diis,

A. Bonifacio IIII., Pontifice,

Deiparoe & S. S. Christi Martyrilus Pio

Dicatum, &c.

"With this single alteration, it serves as exactly for all the purposes of the popish as it did for the pagan worship, for which it was built. For as in the old temple, every one might find the God of his country, and address himself to that deity, whose religion he was most devoted to; so it is the same thing now; every one chooses the patron whom he likes best; and one may see here different services going on at the same time at different altars, with distinct congregations round them, just as the inclinations of the people lead them to the worship of this or that particular saint."—*Dowling's History of Romanism*, page 124.

Papal Rome seems to be as much given to idolatry as ever was pagan Rome. In addition to the veneration of images and pictures, Rome teaches her followers to adore the *relics* of the saints, that is, their *bones, clothing, hair,* &c. No Roman Catholic Church can be *consecrated*, unless some sacred relics are stored in it. It may be a very small relic, a tooth, a toe-nail, a hair, a drop of the blood, or *a preserved tear from the eye;* but so long as it has been declared genuine by the Pope, and placed with the usual ceremonies in the altar of the church, it will suffice. The reverence in which these relics are held is very great, and they even go beyond holy water in their power to work miracles. As every church, in order to be consecrated, must have some relic, the demand for them, and the hunting after them has been immense. It is said that there are as many pieces of the true cross in different parts of Europe, as would supply a town with fuel for an entire winter. We are reminded of the story of the showman, who exhibited the sword with which Balaam smote his ass. The rustic crowd gazed in mute admiration, and the showman was having it all his own way, when a gentleman present called his attention to the fact, that Balaam did not have any sword, but only wished for one. Nothing abashed, the showman replied, " This is the one for which he wished." This certainly was not a very reliable or valuable relic, yet as good as thousands exhibited by the Church of Rome. It is very difficult to see what advantage can be derived from the possession and study of these relics, even if they were all genuine. In what way can the toe-nail of St. Peter, a drop of St. Paul's blood, or some of the beard of John the Baptist, excite our devotion, or make us any holier, even if we are sure that we have them in our possession? But how can we ever know that these old bones, etc., ever did belong to any of the saints? There is no external difference between the bones of St. Paul, and the bones of Judas Iscariot; none between the skull of St. Peter, and that of the impenitent thief. It is true we can get the decision of the Pope. This may satisfy devoted Romanists, but will hardly convince the great outside world. We need not wonder that Roman Catholic countries abound in infidels. Let the Church of Rome pull down its pagan images and pictures, throw away its old bones and other ridiculous relics, and if it does not secure obedience, it may possibly command respect. Having considered the holy water at the door, the images and pictures on the wall, the relics under the altar, we now turn to the priest; (this is the blasphemous name they give to their ministers,) and are at once struck with the strange appearance of his attire. He is dressed in as fantastic a style as though he were a clown in some circus. Joseph's coat of many colors would soon fade if compared with this priestly robe. Now, this may be all right, but it seems difficult to imagine Peter or Paul dressed after such a fashion. Christ declared that God, being a Spirit, must be worshiped "in spirit and in truth." Now no particular kind of dress for ministers is forbidden in the Bible, and none is commanded; but at the same time all this display of pomp and pride seems strangely inconsistent with pure and spiritual worship. In addition to the images and pictures on the wall, the fantastic attire of the priests, the glitter of altar and shrine, we notice at a certain point in the service, clouds of incense floating in the air. This is a purely pagan custom. The use of incense was unknown to the early christians, except as they beheld it in the temples of the heathen. Virgil, speaking of the Paphian Venus, says :

> " Her hundred altars there with garlands crowned,
> And richest incense smoking breathe around
> Sweet odors."—*Æn.* 1, 420.

"Under the pagan emperors, *the use of incense for any purpose of religion was thought so contrary to the obligations of Christianity*, that, in their persecutions, the very method of trying and convicting a Christian, was by requiring him only to throw the least grain of it into the censer, or on the altar. Under the Christian emperors, on the other hand, it was looked upon as a rite *so peculiarly heathenish*, that the very places or houses where it could be proved to have been done, were, by a law of Thedosius, confiscated to the government. In the old *bas-reliefs*, or pieces of sculpture, we never fail to see a boy in a sacred habit, which was always white, attending on the priest, with a little chest or box in his hands, in which this incense was kept for the use of the altar. And in the same manner still, in the Church of Rome, there is always a boy in a surplice waiting on the priest at the altar, with the sacred utensils; among the rest the Thuribulum, or vessel of incense, which the priest, with many ridiculous motions and crossings, waves several times, as it is smoking around and over the altar, in different parts of the service."—*Dowling's History of Romanism, pages* 115, 116.

Candles will also be observed by the curious visitor burning upon the various altars. These are not for the purpose of illumination, as they are kept burning in the day-time. Here we have another innovation upon primitive worship, drawn from the abominations of heathenism. This custom, Herodotus tells us, was first introduced by the Egyptians. Many of the early writers expose the folly of this heathen practice. "*They light up candles to God,*" says Loitontius, "*as if He lived in the dark;* and do they not deserve to pass for madmen who offer lamps to the Author and Giver of light?*"

If any reader of this book doubts the correctness of the account here given of Romish worship, let him step into the nearest Roman Catholic church, and verify the matter for himself. If the images and pictures, the costly robes and glittering altars, the candles, incense and holy water, the operatic music and gay processions, do not remind him of some gorgeous pageant, or heathen temple, we will be very much mistaken. Turning from these matters to the worship itself, we are astonished to hear the priest read the service in a strange and unfamiliar tongue. It is Latin; for this is the language of the Church of Rome. In this dead and, to the masses of the people, forgotten tongue, the Romish service is said. One would think that if an unknown tongue were to be employed, it would be Hebrew or Greek—the language in which the Word of God was first written. But Rome says that Latin is to be preferred — and Rome claims to be infallible. A curse is pronounced upon all who affirm that Mass should be performed in any other tongue. As for our part, we do not see the necessity of performing any part of divine service in any other than the language of the people. Paul says : " In the church I had rather speak five words with my understanding, that by my voice I might teach others also, than ten thousand words in an unknown tongue."—1 Cor. xiv., 19. Not only is the service said in Latin, but by the most of the priests it is so poorly and hurriedly said that the whole thing takes the appearance of a farce. Time would fail to enumerate all the abominations introduced by the Church of Rome in the worship of the pure and holy God. The attention of the people is turned away from the sublime and holy truths of Revelation, and directed to a senseless round of form and ceremony. Rome has poisoned the very fountain of Christian life; for it is by waiting on the Lord (joining in His worship) that Christians renew their strength.

We have already gone over the major part of Romish doctrine, but one awful subversion of sacred truth, one gross abomination, remains to be mentioned. *The Church of Rome says that there are seven sacraments.* We only read of two in the Bible, but the Church of Rome, having tradition to appeal to, and being (in his own estimation) infallible, has added five more.

These five are Confirmation, Penance, Extreme Unction, Holy Order and Matrimony. Confirmation is their ceremony of receiving persons into full communion with the church. The Bishop is the administrator. The candidates kneel before him. A chrism, made of oil of olives and balsam, and consecrated by the bishop, is put on the face of the person in the form of a cross, the bishop saying : " I sign thee with the sign of the cross, and I confirm thee with the chrism of salvation, in the name of the Father, and of the Son, and of the Holy Ghost." A little blow on the cheek is sometimes added. This, they say, is to teach them to bear the trials and persecutions of the world with Christian calmness and fortitude.

Now, if this was *simply* their manner of receiving members into the church, although we should much prefer some other method, we would yet have no controversy with them on the subject, but when they give it sacramental qualities, we feel

compelled to oppose it as unsound and unscriptural. They base it on the laying on of the hands of the apostles, several times mentioned in the New Testament; but this was for the bestowment of special and extraordinary gifts. The gifts have ceased, and therefore the ceremony. "Every sacrament must have its appointment from Christ, consisting both of an outward sign and words of institution. But this ordinance of theirs has none of these. The sign which they use is oil. Their words of consecration are, ' I sign thee with the sign of the cross, anoint thee with the chrism of health, in the name of the Father, and of the Son, and of the Holy Ghost.' But none of these have their institution from Christ or his apostles. We read, indeed, that the apostles used imposition of hands, but never of chrism or oil. Indeed, this superstitious device was not then in use, being brought in long after by Sylvester, who is reported by Damascus to have been the deviser of chrism."
—*Elliot on Romanism, pages* 232–233.

Penance is the performance of some task given by the priest in confession, (as the saying of so many *Ave Marias* or *Pater Nosters*), by which satisfaction is made for sin. This matter of confession and the true method of obtaining pardon, has already been gone over. Jesus Christ died for all men, and all who will may obtain pardon through faith in him. Nothing that we can do, will add to the perfect work of Calvary. Extreme Unction is the *funniest* ceremony in the Church of Rome. There is nothing funny in the occasion, for it is given to those about to die, but the *idea* of anointing the body of a dying man, in order to help him elude the grasp of the Devil, is supremely ridiculous. The ceremony consists in anointing the dying man with oil that has been blessed by the bishop, the oil being applied to the *eyes, ears, nose,* mouth, hands, and sometimes to the *kidneys.* Now, where is the scriptural foundation for all this? We are pointed, it is true, to the case mentioned by St. James, but the anointing in this case was given with reference to the cure of the sick man, whereas Romanists never give extreme unction while there remains any hope of life. The anointing practiced by the apostles was the attendant and token of a miraculous cure. These *miraculous* recoveries have ceased, and why should we continue the sign? The two remaining of the added sacraments are Orders and Matrimony. How unscriptural it is to place them among the sacraments, we will leave the Bible-loving reader to determine.

The pen tires, and the heart sickens in recounting the abominations of which Rome is the prolific mother. The author well remembers a remark made to him by the late lamented Dr. Mattison. "If," said he, "all the devils in Hell had been at work for a thousand years to devise a system of falsehood and iniquity, they could have prepared nothing better suited to their purpose than Romanism." Romanism perverts Scripture truth, exalts the Father and tradition as of equal authority, denies the right of private interpretation, turns the worship of God into childish mockery, and, whenever possible, persecutes even unto death all who will not bow to her ghostly authority. Her bishops and chief pastors, convened in general council, curse the progress of the age, bewail the prevalence of civil and religious liberty, and would, if they could, put back the world into the darkness of the middle ages. Like certain deadly plants, Popery thrives best in darkness and in gloom. The light of progress and liberty will bring death to her dark and deep designs. Let the people have the light of knowledge—let them learn to reason for themselves—and the power of Rome will be forever broken.

I will conclude this chapter by referring to one more of the abominations of Romanism. I mean the pretended power of working miracles. This power was given to the apostles as the credentials of the correctness of their message and the reality of their commission. As the church became established, and received for a guide the New Testament, miracles gradually disappeared, and soon ceased to exist at all. This power the Roman Catholic Church has never ceased to claim. If, however, we examine her boasted miracles by the usual tests, they soon disappear. The miracles of the Bible are dignified and beneficent. The miracles of Romanism are absurd in the highest degree. The miracles of the Bible are well attested by competent witnesses. The miracles of Romanism are unattested, except by those pretending to effect them. A few of them may be named for the amusement of the reader. *Dogs, asses* and *bees*, for the benefit and conversion of heretics, have adored the sacred host. Many miracles are ascribed to St. Dominic. A knight, to whom he presented a rosary, became so holy that every time he dropped a bead he beheld an angel convey it to the Virgin Mary, who magnified it, and with the whole string built a palace upon a mountain in Paradise. When Dominic entered the city of Thoulouse, all the bells of the city rang to welcome him, untouched by human hands. *When a nursing babe he regularly observed fast days, and would get out of bed and lie upon the ground as a penance.* They will show you at Loretto, in Naples, a house in which the Virgin Mary is said to have been born; and will gravely inform you that this house was carried *through the air by angels,* from Nazareth to Loretto, a few centuries ago.

Our whole book might be filled with these absurd, "lying wonders," and thousands yet would remain untold.

Is not Rome well called the "Mother of harlots and abominations of the earth"? No name is too harsh for such a monster of iniquity. There may be words in the English language strong enough to express our indignation and contempt for this vile system of shame and wrong, but we cannot now recall them.

So, blessing the memory of honest Martin Luther, and praying that author and reader may alike be kept secure from the machinations of the "Man of Sin," we bring this chapter to its close.

CHAPTER XIV.

DRUNK WITH BLOOD.

" *And I saw the woman drunken with the blood of the Saints, and with the blood of the martyrs of Jesus.*" REV. xvii 6.

" Such are the tender mercies, tyrant Rome !
The rack, the faggot, or the hated creed—
Fearless amid thy folds fierce wolves may roam,
Whilst stainless sheep upon thy altars bleed."

FROM the commencement of her history, up to the present time, Rome has been distinguished by a cruel and blood-thirsty spirit. Millions of our fellow-beings have met with death at her hands. These bloody and terrible persecutions have not been exceptions to an otherwise peaceful history; but the steady and unvarying practice of the church. It is the *doctrine* of the Romish Church, that heretics may be persecuted even unto death. Cardinal Bellarmine is the great expounder of Romish doctrines. In the

21st and 22d chapters of the third book of his work, entitled "De Laias," (concerning the laity,) he boldly claims for the church, the right of punishing heretics with death. The notes in the Rhemish Testament teach the same horrid doctrine. The comment on Luke ix., 55, reads as follows: "Not justice, nor all rigorous punishment of sinners, is here forbidden; nor Elias's fact reprehended; nor the Church, nor Christian princes, blamed for putting heretics to death; but that none of these should be done for desire of our particular revenge, or without discretion, and in regard of their amendment and example to others." In the celebrated work of Peter Dens, a text-book in nearly every popish college and seminary, we find the following on this subject: "Are heretics *rightly punished* with Death? St. Thomas rightly answers in the affirmative. Because forgers of money, or other disturbers of the state, are justly punished with death; therefore also heretics, who are forgers of the faith, and, as experience shows, greatly disturb the state. * * * This is confirmed by the command of God, under the old law, that the false prophets should be killed. * * * The same is proved by the condemnation—by the fourteenth article, of John Huss, in the Council of Constance." Thus the reader will see that this is still the doctrine of the Romish Church. They have not the power to put this doctrine in practice, as they once had, but should (God forbid) this power ever return to them again, we have no reason to expect anything else than a return to the bloody persecutions of the past. It has been estimated that from the birth of Popery, in 606, to the present time, more than *Fifty Millions* of our race, have been slain by this Monster of Iniquity. This is an average of more than 40,000 for every year of the existence of Popery.

"No computation can reach the numbers who have been put to death, in different ways, on account of their maintaining the profession of the Gospel, and opposing the corruptions of the Church of Rome. A million of poor Waldenses perished in France; nine hundred thousand orthodox Christians were slain in less than thirty years after the institution of the order of the Jesuits. The Duke of Alva boasted of having put to death, in the Netherlands, thirty-six thousand, by the hand of the common executioner, during the space of a few years. These are a few specimens, and but a few, of those which history has recorded; but the total amount will never be known till the earth shall disclose her blood, and no more cover her slain."—(*Scott's Church History.*) The persecutions of pagan Rome dwindle into insignificance, when compared with the persecutions of papal Rome.

England, now a peaceful, happy Protestant country, has been the scene of many a fierce Romish persecution. During the reign of the " Bloody Queen Mary," a space of five years, 288 persons were burned at the stake, for the crime of loving Jesus and the blessed Bible. The first martyr was the venerable John Rogers, who was burned at Smithfield on the 4th of February, 1555. The martyrdom of Saunders and Hooper, of Taylor and Bradford, of Latimer, of Ridley, and Cranmer, soon followed. The death of Cranmer was a very remarkable one. In a moment of weakness, when threatened with a cruel and violent death, he placed his signature to a written recantation. He lived to bitterly repent of this act, and died at the stake, thus, like thousands of others, sealing his testimony with his blood. As the flames rose up around him, he held forth his right hand and said: ".This is the hand that wrote it, and therefore it shall suffer punishment first." He died in glorious triumph.

God can make human wrath result in his own glory and the good of his children. So was it at this time. Queen Mary soon after died, and peace was restored to the unhappy land. The people had seen enough of Romanism. The Protestants of *France*, although they enjoy a fair degree of religious liberty now, have suffered many severe persecutions in the past. Who has not heard of the massacre of St. Bartholomew? Romanists wish that it might be forgotten, but unrelenting history has carefully preserved the record of it. It took place on the 24th of August, 1572. It began and raged most extensively at Paris, yet extended throughout the kingdom. The plan was laid by the queen-dowager of France, Catharine de Medici, in concert with her son, Charles IX. Under the pretext of a marriage between Henry, the Protestant king of Navarre, and Margaret, the sister of Charles, the Protestants, in vast numbers, had been attracted to Paris. At midnight the signal was given, and the butchery commenced. No human language can set forth the horrors of that frightful massacre. For several days the streets of Paris ran with blood. Some ten thousand persons, of every age and sex, were murdered. From Paris the slaughter extended throughout the kingdom, and nearly 100,000 Protestants fell as victims to papal cruelty. Solemn thanks were returned to God for so signal a victory. Medals were ordered to be coined to perpetuate its memory. The news of this fearful murder was received at Rome with unrestrained delight. A universal jubilee was proclaimed by the Pope.

The guns of St. Angelo were fired, and bonfires lighted in the streets. A medal was struck in the Pope's mint, with his own head on one side, and a representation of the massacre on the other, with an angel brandishing a sword, bearing the inscription: "*Hugonotarum Strages*," overthrow of the Huguenots.

In the year 1598, twenty-six years after this horrid massacre, Henry IV. issued an edict granting the Protestants liberty of worship. In 1685 Louis XIV. revoked this edict, and the old persecutions were revived. They were not allowed to assemble for public worship, their ministers were banished, and their children compelled to go to Romish churches. A common mode of punishment was called *dragooning*, that is, quartering brutal dragoons upon the poor Protestants.

These dragoons could torture the defenceless people in any way they pleased. Dowling, in his very able history, gives the following extract on this matter, from Quick's Synodicom: "There was no wickedness, though ever so brutal, which they did not put in practice, that they might enforce them to change their religion. Amidst a thousand hideous cries and blasphemies, they hung up men and women by the hair or feet upon the roofs of their chambers, or hooks of chimneys, and smoked them with wisps of wet hay till they were no longer able to bear it; and when they had taken them down, if they would not sign an abjuration of their pretended heresies, they then trussed them up again immediately. Some they threw into great fires, kindled on purpose, and would not take them out till they were half roasted. They tied ropes under their arms, and plunged them again and again into deep wells, from whence they would not draw them till they had promised to change their religion. They bound them as criminals are when they are put to the rack, and in that posture, putting a funnel into their mouths, they poured wine down their throats till its fumes had deprived them of their reason, and they had in that condition made them consent to become Catholics. Some they stripped stark naked, and after they had offered them a thousand indignities, they stuck them with pins from head to foot; they cut them with penknives, tore them by the noses with red-hot pincers, and dragged them about the rooms till they promised to become Roman Catholics, or till the doleful cries of these poor tormented creatures, calling upon God for mercy, constrained them to let them go. They beat them with staves, and dragged them, all bruised, to the Popish churches, where their enforced presence is reputed for an abjuration. They kept them working seven or eight days together, relieving one another by turns, that they might not get a wink of sleep or rest. In case they began to nod, they threw buckets of water in their faces, or, holding kettles over their heads, they beat on them with such a continual noise that those poor wretches lost their senses. If they found any sick, who kept their beds, men or women, be it of fevers or other diseases, they were so cruel as to beat up an alarm with twelve drums about their beds for a whole week together, without intermission, till they had promised to change. In some places they tied husbands and fathers to the bed-posts, and ravished their wives and daughters before their eyes. And in other places rapes were publicly and generally permitted for hours together. From others they plucked off the nails of their hands and toes, which must needs have caused an intolerable pain."

The heart sickens at the review of these horrid details. After all, the half has not been told us. Much will never be known until the awful day of judgment shall reveal all the secrets of earth. We will briefly refer to the persecutions of the Waldenses. This peaceful and virtuous people lived in the south of France and in Piedmont. They would never bow to the dictum of the Pope, or follow the corrupt teachings of the Roman Catholic Church. For this they suffered the most terrible and protracted persecutions. Popish armies again and again laid waste their happy homes. Children were torn from the arms of loving parents, that they might be reared under Roman Catholic influence. The helpless victims of papal cruelty suffered death in a thousand different forms. Some, like the saints of old, were sawn asunder. Some had their throats cut. Others were hurled from the top of some lofty clift. Neither old age nor helpless infancy could provoke pity.

Let those who regard the Romish hierarchy as a branch of Christ's true church, and who love to imitate her ways and teachings, seriously ponder on these bloody persecutions. If ever Popery gets control of this land, we may expect to see these awful scenes re-enacted.

It is true, these horrid transactions are a thing of the past, but when have they been repudiated? They never have been, and never will be. The Church of Rome claims to be infallible, and having set her seal to these enormities, dare not go back on her past history.

Again we affirm, that all Rome wants is the power. Her teachings are unchanged, her spirit as stern and cruel as ever. Her garments are stained with the blood of fifty million saints, and she still thirsts for more. Let us not flatter ourselves that the spirit of Rome has been tamed, or her thirst for blood quenched. It will be time enough to believe this, when she shows sorrow for her past deeds of blood and cruelty. We must see to it that her persecutions are over, in this land of Freedom, at least. We must not trust to honeyed words and soft pretences. If we warm the viper, we will surely be bitten. Prevention is better than cure. God helping us, we will never allow Romanism to establish her infernal Inquisition on American soil.

CHAPTER XV.

ROME IN PROPHECY.

"*Now the Spirit speaketh expressly, that in the latter times some shall depart from the faith, giving heed to seducing spirits, and doctrines of devils; speaking lies in hypocrisy, having their conscience seared with a hot iron; forbidding to marry, and commanding to abstain from meats, which God hath created to be received with thanksgiving of them which believe and know the truth.*"—1 TIM. iv. 1–3.

MAN has always manifested an intense desire to know the future. History acquaints him with the past, and his faculties of observation give him a knowledge of the present; yet still he loves to peer into the shadowy future, and often anxiously inquires concerning "Things coming on the earth." This desire God has, in a measure, been pleased to gratify. He has, in his Holy Word, to some extent, lifted the vail concealing the future, and revealed to us a grand outline of all human history. It is true, that all parts of prophecy are not fully understood, and perhaps will not be, until the events predicted shall have taken place; much seems dim and uncertain, yet still much can be understood. We see that truth is to triumph over evil and error, and that the glory of God is one day to cover all the earth. No one, it seems to me, can read the Bible without perceiving that a terrible and fearfully wicked power was to arise, hold sway over the earth, and persecute the saints of the Most High for many weary centuries, and finally to disappear beneath the wrath of Almighty God. "Man of Sin," "Anti-Christ," "Babylon," "Great Whore," seem to refer to the same sinful and cruel power, though representing it under different images. These prophetic terms, together with many other names and images, all refer, we think, to the same anti-christian and persecuting hierarchy—*Papal Rome.* The coming of this monster system of iniquity, is first shadowed forth in the 7th chapter of Daniel. This chapter contains an account of a vision, in which the prophet beheld four beasts rising up in succession, and holding dominion over the earth. An explanation of the vision is also furnished us in the same chapter. By comparing this vision, and its explanation, with Nebuchadnezzar's vision of the image, described in the 2d chapter of Daniel, and the prophet's explanation, it will be seen that both visions refer to the same line of events. The four different parts of the image, and the four beasts, represent the four great universal Kingdoms of the earth.

No student of history need be informed that these four kingdoms are the Chaldean or Babylonian, the Medo-Persian, the Grecian, and the Latin or Roman. This last universal kingdom, the Roman, is represented by a beast more terrible and fierce than any of the others. "After this I saw in the night visions, and behold a fourth beast, dreadful and terrible, and strong exceedingly; and it had great iron teeth: it devoured and brake in pieces, and stamped the residue with the feet of it: and it was diverse from all the beasts that were before it; and it had ten horns."—Dan. vii., 7. Nor is this all. From among the ten horns, another, a "little horn" arises and plucks up three of the first horns by the roots. "And behold in this horn were eyes like the eyes of a man, and a mouth speaking great things."

In the latter part of the chapter, this part of the vision is fully explained. "Thus he said, The fourth beast shall be the fourth kingdom upon earth, which shall be diverse from all kingdoms, and shall devour the whole earth, and shall tread it down, and break it in pieces. And the ten horns out of this kingdom are ten kings that shall arise; and another shall arise after them; and he shall be diverse from the first, and he shall subdue three kings. And he shall speak great words against the Most High, and shall wear out the saints of the Most High, and think to change times and laws; and they shall be given into his hand until a time and times and the dividing of time. But the judgment shall sit, and they shall take away his dominion, to consume and to destroy it unto the end."—*Verses* 25, 26.

The fourth beast was different from the other

three, and the Roman was different from all other kingdoms in its republican form of government, its greatness, length of duration, and extent of dominion. This fourth beast is represented as treading down and devouring the whole earth. The protracted wars, bloody conquests, and universal dominion of the Roman Empire, are all matters of history. It was finally divided into ten kingdoms, represented by the ten horns. The list of the ten kingdoms rising up out of the dissolution of the old Roman Empire, as given by Bishop Newton, is as follows: 1. The Senate of Rome, who revolted from the Greek emperors, and claimed, and exerted, the privilege of choosing a new Western emperor. 2. The Greeks in Revenna. 3. The Lombards in Lombardy. 4. The Huns in Hungary. 5. The Alemannes in Germany. 6. The Franks in France. 7. The Burgundians in Burgundy. 8. The Goths in Spain. 9. The Britons. 10. The Saxons in Britain. And now, after, or behind (that is, unperceived by them), arises another kingdom, represented by the little horn, and one diverse from all the others.

"This is generally agreed, by all Protestant interpreters, to be the kingdom of the Pope, which was certainly of a very different nature from any of the former, being first ecclesiastical, or spiritual, and afterward claiming a temporal, or civil jurisdiction."—*Benson.*

Three of the ten kingdoms were to be plucked up by this arrogant new-comer; and history informs us that in the eighth century the exarchate of Revenna, the kingdom of the Lombards, and the state of Rome, were reduced to papal dominion. This little horn "had eyes, and a mouth that spake very great things," and a look "*more stout than his fellows.*"

These eyes denote craft, and cunning, qualities for which Popery has ever been noted. Certainly, if we consider the bulls, anathemas, and absolutions of the various Popes, we shall not have much trouble in finding the "Mouth that spake very great things." This horn was also to "speak great words against" or as "the Most High." This is being fulfilled at the present hour. The old Pope, Pius IX., claims for himself, and his fellow popes, the attribute of infallibility, a matter that belongs only to God. In Gration's Decretals, the title of God is given to the pope; while to-day he is hailed as "O, Lord, our God, the Pope." This hostile power should also "wear out the saints of the Most High;" and the frequent and bloody persecutions of Rome, remind us that this prediction has been more than fulfilled. It should also "Think to change time and laws." This Rome has done in "Appointing fasts and feasts, canonizing saints, granting pardons and indulgences for sins, instituting new modes of worship, imposing new articles of faith, enjoining new rules of practice, and reversing at pleasure the laws of God and man."—*Bishop Newton.* For a long time this proud horn will exercise dominion, but some day "The judgment shall sit, and they shall take away his dominion, to consume and to destroy it unto the end." Christ must finally triumph, and his Kingdom will sooner or later overcome all opposition. Popery will perish, and the Kingdom of Emanuel arise in everlasting beauty upon its ruins.

Passing on now to the New Testament, we have in the second epistle of Paul to the Thessalonians a very full prediction of the papal dominion and enormities. "Let no man deceive you by any means: for that day shall not come, except there come a falling away first, and that man of sin be revealed, the son of perdition; who opposeth and exalteth himself above all that is called God, or that is worshipped, so that he, as God, sitteth in the temple of God, shewing himself that he is God. * * * * * And then shall that wicked be revealed, whom the Lord shall consume with the spirit of his mouth, and shall destroy with the brightness of his coming: even him, whose coming is after the working of Satan, with all power, and signs, and lying wonders, and with all deceivableness of unrighteousness in them that perish; because they received not the love of the truth, that they might be saved.

"And for this cause God shall send them strong delusion, that they should believe a lie:

"That they all might be damned who believed not the truth, but had pleasure in unrighteousness."

Nothing has ever appeared in the history of the world to which this description applies so well, as to Popery. Unless we apply them thus, it seems well nigh impossible to give them any meaning whatever. Those who compare this chapter with the 7th of Daniel, will see a wonderful resemblance between the two. In some verses Paul seems to be almost quoting the precise language of his brother prophet.

Some false teachers had persuaded the Thessalonians that the day of judgment was nigh at hand. As the result of this teaching, many of them had indulged in great folly, going so far in some cases as to neglect their usual business, and ceasing to make any further provision for their families. Paul wrote his second epistle that he might bring them back to a sound mind, and restore the Church to its former healthy condition. He tells them that before the end of the world shall come, there will be a fearful apostasy from the truth, a dark and stormy period for the true followers of Christ. He warns them that already the unholy leaven has commenced to work. Germs of false doctrine and practice have been sown, from which shall spring up a corrupt and blood-red harvest.

By the "Man of sin" we do not think that any one pope is meant, but the whole succession of boastful deceivers. The term "king" is sometimes used in Scripture for a whole succession of kings. The term high-priest is used (Heb. ix., 7, 25,) for the series and order of high-priests. So we think the term "Man of sin" is used to designate the whole line of unholy, cruel, arrogant and vicious men, that have occupied for so many centuries the pretended chair of St. Peter.

Having gone over the predictions of Daniel relative to the Papacy somewhat in detail, we need not dwell very long on the chapter before us. Allusion has already been made to the high claims and blasphemous titles of the Popes. They have seemed to take special pains that the 4th verse of the chapter before us should not lack for fulfillment. The "signs and lying wonders" are worthy a brief consideration. For these Romanism has ever been noted. The "Lives of Saints," so popular among Roman Catholics, are full of the most ridiculous stories. The "Breviary," which every priest must read for nearly two hours every day, is stuffed with narrations of a like character. One of them may be given as a sample of the rest. A saint had his head nearly cut off by some wicked person, yet he lived two days, and carried it in his hands two miles across the country, and laid it down where a church was afterwards built.

Many other examples of a like character might be given. Who can tell but that the period of Rome's "strong delusion" has now fully come, and that the lie to which they are given over is none other than the dogma of Papal Infallibility?

Paul, in his first epistle to Timothy, refers again to the coming apostasy. His words have been placed at the head of this chapter. It was a "*departure from the faith,*" that Paul foretold, and this answers exactly to Romanism. The little society of believers, gathered at Rome in the time of the apostles, was so pure, that their faith was "spoken of throughout the whole world." But, one corruption crept in after another, power and wealth completed the work, and the pure faith of Christ was banished from Rome, leaving the "Mother of Harlots" enthroned mistress of the world. This apostasy was to "*give heed to seducing spirits;*" and thus has papal Rome long been doing. She prays to saints and angels, claims to know the exact condition of the departed, and enforces her pretended revelations by claiming angelic visions and visitants. "*And doctrines of devils,*" or rather, doctrines concerning demons. The *demons* of the Greeks were beings of a middle nature between God and man. To these they prayed and gave worship as mediators.

The doctrine and practice of Rome concerning the supposed mediatorship of saints and angels, agrees very fully with the doctrine of the ancient Greeks concerning demons. "*Speaking lies in hypocrisy.*" How well this accords with the character of the Romish priesthood, those who know much about them can soon decide. These lies seem to be spoken especially in establishing the doctrine of demons, that is, the worship of saints and angels. "It is impossible," says Bishop Newton, "to relate or enumerate all the various falsehoods and lies which have been invented and propagated for this purpose; the fabulous books, forged under the names of apostles, saints and martyrs; the fabulous legends of their lives, actions, sufferings and deaths; the fabulous miracles ascribed to their sepulchres, bones, and other relics; the fabulous dreams and revelations, visions, and apparitions of the dead to the living; and even the fabulous saints, who never existed but in the imaginations of their worshipers; and all these stories the monks, the priests, the bishops of the church, have imposed and obtruded upon mankind, it is difficult to say, whether with greater artifice or cruelty, with greater confidence or hypocrisy, and pretended sanctity, a more hardened face, or a more hardened conscience."

"*Having their consciences seared with a hot iron.*" Of course, no man could set forth lies so great in number and dark in guilt, unless the conscience was thus seared. "*Forbidding to marry.*" Papal Rome has long forbidden marriage to her clergy, and exalted celibacy as a holier state. "*And commanding to abstain from meats.*" Rome forbids the use of animal food to some men at all times, and to all men at certain times.

Well has Dr. Hatfield, speaking of the predictions we have been considering, said: "It is almost impossible to read these words without a conviction, or at least a suspicion, that they were written for the express purpose of describing the apostate Church of Rome."

John, in his epistles, speaks of an "Anti-Christ." The Greek word means instead of, as well as opposed to. The anti-popes claimed papal authority for themselves, and opposed the reigning pontiff. Anti-Christ likewise means one opposed to Christ, and also claiming the titles and power of Christ. Able interpreters agree that Anti-Christ denotes an organized body of men, perpetuated from age to age, opposed to Christ, and which he will destroy.

Where can we look for the fulfillment of this prophecy, if it is not fulfilled in the Popedom? The identity of papal Rome with Anti-Christ has been maintained by Luther, Calvin, Zwingli, Melancthon, Bucer, Beza, Bengel, Cranmer, Latimer, Ridley, Hooper, Tyndale, Rogers, Sir Isaac Newton, Mede, Bishop Newton, Louth, Vitringa, D'Aubigne, Gaussen, Ouseley, Dowling, Mattison, and a host of other able thinkers, both in this country and Europe.

We will now turn to the 13th chapter of Revelations. The Book of Revelations is the most mysterious in the Bible. It is full of types, shadows, and symbols. Much of it is not perhaps at this time fully understood. Still, we are not to turn away from it, as from a book hopelessly sealed. A blessing is pronounced upon those who read and understand it. It is a part of Scripture, and is therefore " Given by inspiration of God," and designed for our comfort and instruction. Moreover, the author in presenting a few thoughts to the reader, concerning the part Romanism plays in the grand apocalyptic vision, is not giving the result of independent research, but the views of some of the ablest and most sober commentators. In the 13th chapter of Revelations, John tells us that he beheld two beasts, one rising up from the sea, and the other coming out of the earth. These two beasts, we think, represent Romanism, the first representing its secular, and the second its ecclesiastical power. It claims to be supreme in both. The first beast came up out of the sea, that is, from the midst of war and tumult, and had seven heads and ten horns. The great mass of commentators, ancient and modern, Protestants and Papists, agree in maintaining that this beast represents the Roman Empire. The only question is whether it represents pagan

Rome, or Rome under the Popes. It must mean Rome under the Popes, for the pagan Roman empire rose and was established long before St. John's time. The seven heads may allude to the seven mountains, on which the city of Rome is built, or to the seven forms of government which successively prevailed there. The ten horns signify the ten Kingdoms, into which the Roman empire was divided. This has already been considered. " The names of blasphemy " may refer to the idolatrous names applied to the city of Rome, such as " *The Eternal City,*" " The heavenly city," etc. This beast is the same as Daniel's fourth beast. It partakes, however, of the qualities of the three former beasts, having the form of a leopard, the feet of a bear, and the mouth of a lion.

Many of the evils of the Grecian, Persian, and Babylonian empires were perpetuated in the Roman. To this new form of the Roman empire, the dragon, old pagan Rome, gave "his power, and his seat, and great authority." One of the seven heads was "wounded unto death." This appears to have been the sixth head, for five were fallen before St. John's time. (See chap. xvii., 10.) The five fallen heads, or forms of government, were kings, consuls, dictators, decemvirs, and military tribunes. The sixth head, or the power of the emperors, was wounded unto death, when the Roman empire was overturned by the invasion of the northern nations, and the name and office of emperor alike destroyed. This "deadly wound was healed" when the pope and people of Rome revolted from the exarch of Ravenna, and proclaimed Charles the Great emperor of the Romans. This beast is represented as speaking great things, blaspheming God, persecuting the saints, and holding almost universal sway over the nations of the earth.

This the secular empire did, *yet, under the control and by the dictation of the ecclesiastical power.* Roman Catholic writers have sometimes boasted that the Church never claimed the power of slaying heretics; it could only give them over to the civil power. We all know just what that means.

As well might the assassin affirm that he did not do the fatal deed, but the knife that he held in his hand. And now (verse 11) the prophet beholds another beast. This beast rises up out of the earth, that is, like a plant, silently, without at first attracting much attention, and has two horns like a lamb. This beast represents, we think, the ecclesiastical power of papal Rome. Although this beast had the appearance of a lamb, he nevertheless " spake as a dragon." The Romish Church pretends to be very meek and holy, yet commands and slays like a tyrant. This second beast joined in concerted action with the first. The secular and ecclesiastical power of Rome go hand in hand. We do not hear so much of the former now, simply because they dare not exercise it. We have no doubt that if Romanism ever gets control of national affairs again, we shall hear the same lordly pretentions and the same stern decrees, absolving subjects from allegiance to their government, and giving states and crowns to parties pleasing to the " Mother Church."

Verse 13th refers to the pretended miracles of Romanism, to which reference has been made already. "And he doeth great wonders, so that he maketh fire come down from heaven on the earth in the sight of men."

By means of these pretended miracles the nations of the earth have been deceived, and the power of Popery extended far and wide. "And deceiveth them that dwell on the earth by means of those miracles which he had the power to do in the sight of the beast, saying to them that dwell on the earth, that they should make an image to the beast, which had the wound of a sword, and did live. And he had power to give life unto the image of the beast, that the image of the beast should both speak, and cause that as many as would not worship the image of the beast should be killed."—*Verses* 14, 15. This image of the beast, this *representative idol*, many have supposed to be the Pope. He is only a private person until the two-horned beast, the ecclesiastical power, select him and consecrate him as pope. He is then adored as the vicar of Christ, and millions have suffered death because they would not join in this idolatry.

The two-horned beast is further represented as causing all men to receive in the hand or forehead some mark, by which his ownership of them might be publicly acknowledged. Those who had not this mark could neither buy nor sell. Rome, whenever possessed of the power, has always caused men to bow down to her peculiar forms, and has often interdicted from buying or selling those who would not comply.

The reader is referred for further light on the history and destiny of Popery to the 17th and 18th chapters of the book of Revelations. In one chapter it is represented under the figure of a harlot; in the other under that of a wicked and populous city. But the harlot is to be judged, and the city to be overthrown. The Bible clearly marks out the rise, progress, sway and final overthrow of Romanism. Its days are numbered. Already there are signs of the coming ruin. The entire edifice is rotten, and must fall. It is crimsoned by the blood and reeking with the moral filth of ages, and soon the thunderbolts of Divine wrath shall cleave it from cap-stone to foundation. The twelve hundred and sixty days are hastening to their close. The Pope is propped up by French bayonets, and when they are withdrawn the Italians will hurl him in indignation from the throne. I hope that reader and writer will live to see the hour. It seems to me that the skies will be brighter, and the light sweeter, and that men will breathe freer, when the dark shadow of Popery is lifted from the earth.

CHAPTER XVI.

THE PERIL OF THE HOUR.

"To be forewarned is to be forearmed."—*Old Proverb.*

OUR task is well-nigh done. We have endeavored to state fairly the questions at issue between Romanists and Protestants. We have demonstrated the right of the Bible, and the Bible alone, to decide in this, and all other controversies of a religious character. We have shown how Popery arose, and have carefully considered its false dogmas and superstitious practices. We have followed the stream of her dark and bloody history, until we turned with horror from the theme. We have viewed the prophetic relations of Romanism, and have read of its corrupt history and final overthrow in the Word of God. It now only remains that we warn our countrymen of its dark and deep designs concerning our beloved land, and of the fearful shadow hanging over this fair republic. Casting a hurried glance over the nations of the earth, we see that in many lands Romanism is going down. It is going down in Spain, in Mexico, in Austria, in France—yea, in Italy itself. Bibles are now distributed in Rome, and more than this, thanks to Victor Emanuel, Protestant churches have been organized in that city. Spain has been, in like manner, thrown open to the light, and the pure gospel of Christ may now be preached in that once benighted land. In Austria the Pope has been openly defied, and a faint gleam of religious liberty breaks in upon that land, so long held in complete subjection to the Papal See. In Mexico a small band of believers have organized the "Church of Jesus," in opposition to the corrupt Church of Rome, called in that land the "Church of Mary."

While Romanism is thus going down in the Old World, and even in some parts of the New, it is *on the increase* in the United States. It presents the phenomenon of a tree dead or dying in the trunk and branches, yet sending up a green and vigorous shoot from the roots. The old Pope sees that his power is waning in Europe, and longs to establish his tottering throne on a firmer basis in the United States. The Romish press and priesthood already begin to boast that this country will soon be theirs. Father Hecker has predicted that such an event will be brought to pass within the next thirty years. He may be bolder and more hopeful than some of his colleagues, but they all look forward to the time when this republic shall be completely under their control.

Any one by comparing the strength of Rome in the United States, at the present time, with its strength and position ten years ago, will see that during the past ten years it has made fearful progress. If we want to know what will be our position, if Rome ever gets supreme control in this land, we can soon satisfy our curiosity. We know what Romanism has been in the ages past. We tremble as we read her dark and bloody history. We know what Romanism is to-day. We hear the same lordly pretensions, and every now and then, see the manifestations of her cruel and intolerant spirit. We know what Romanism is in Spain, in Austria, in Mexico, in Ireland, in Italy. We know how much religious liberty was enjoyed at Rome, when the Pope was supreme, and the influence of Protestantism was unfelt; in Rome, where Protestant worship was forbidden by law, and American women arrested for seeking to found an orphan asylum. No Protestant Englishman or Scotchman dare buy land in any part of Romish Ireland with a view to living on it. Here is the notice, which not long ago was served on many Protestant landlords and tenants in the Romish districts of Ireland:

"NOTICE!
MARCH, 1869.

"SIR:—*You have let to a heretic, or Protestant, a farm in this part of the country, but he shall never put his foot upon it, or he will never leave it alive. We will never allow a heretic to live amongst us. So if he put his foot on these lands he will be shot dead. The ball is ready for him. This is no idle threat, so help me God.*

"ONE OF THE PEOPLE."

This spirit Romanists bring with them to this

country. A fine illustration was given of it, a short time ago, in the city of New York, when a peaceful pic-nic, held under the auspices of the "American Protestant Association," was violently assailed and broken up. These things are not done by the people without the knowledge and connivance of the priests and leaders. They have the people under their complete control, and *could prevent these scenes of blood, if they only wished to. If they can keep them from reading Protestant books, and going to Protestant churches, they can keep them from assailing Protestant pic-nics and mobbing Protestant lecturers.*

Once in a while some of their leaders are rash enough to lift the curtain and show us the dark and fearful background. Some years ago the *Shepherd of the Valley*, the organ of the Bishop of St. Louis, gave expression to the following sentiment: "The Church is, of necessity, intolerant. Heresy she endures when and where she must; but she hates it, and directs all her energies to its destruction. If Catholics ever gain an immense numerical majority, religious freedom in this country is at an end. So our enemies say; so we believe." Brownson's *Review*, of about the same date, joins in substantially the same assertion: "The liberty of heresy and unbelief is not a natural right. All the rights the *sects* have, or can have, are derived from the State, and rest on *expediency*. As they have, in their character of sects hostile to the true religion (Popery), no rights under the law of nature or the law of God, they are neither wronged nor deprived of liberty, if the State refuses to grant them any rights at all." The New York *Tablet* ridicules the idea of a "liberal Catholic." A Western Roman Catholic paper recently said: "Heresy and unbelief are crimes, and in states under religious (Romish) control, are to be punished as other crimes."

A very important question now arises, namely: By what means does Romanism hope to get the supremacy in this country? She has more than one method of reaching this point. Her plans are deep and well laid. Some of them we will now consider.

1. *She hopes to destroy our public school system, and thus increase her power, by quenching this torch of light and learning.*

The more ignorant and superstitious a community is, the better can Romanism work among it. A mad dog does not dread the sight of water any worse than a Roman Catholic priest dreads the sight of a public school. Some think that Romanists will be satisfied if they can get the Bible out of the public schools, but such is not the case. Nothing will satisfy them but the complete abolition of the entire system.

On this point the Roman Catholic press is decided and united. The *Tablet* says: "To us godless schools are still less acceptable than sectarian schools; and we object less to the reading of King James' Bible, even in the schools, than we do to the exclusion of all religious instruction."

The *Catholic World* says: "We oppose separating secular training from religious training, and can never consent to the secularization of education. Here is where we and the present race of Protestants differ. It is because the common schools secularize, and are intended by their chief supporters to secularize, education, and to make all life secular, that we oppose them, and refuse to send our children to them, when we can possibly avoid it."

It is easy to see the drift of these remarks. They want the schools under the dominion of Romanism, or else they want the entire system abolished. They do not wish to join in supporting them, and they refuse to send their children to them. Our glorious public school system stands as a mighty barrier before the advancing waves of Romanism. Remove this barrier, and their final victory will become a mere question of time.

2. *They hope to make a host of youthful converts by means of their convents and sectarian schools.*

They have a vast number of schools and seminaries scattered all over the land. They make great pretensions, and many silly Protestants send their sons and daughters to be educated in them. It is so fashionable and romantic to go away to the "College of the Sacred Heart," "St. Joseph's

Academy," or the "Ursuline Convent," to be educated. Poor, red-faced, ignorant Mrs. Shoddy, who thinks that "one church is as good as another," and who does not know but that the massacre of St. Bartholomew took place during the late war, thinks that it is such a fine thing to say, "My daughter has been educated in a convent." Poor, silly flies! so easily trapped by the Romish spiders. These academies and seminaries are grand proselyting institutions. *They are the poorest schools in the country.* They give a little smattering of French and music, painting and drawing; but as for history, science, literature, but little is taught or learned. They teach silly and romantic young women how to become Roman Catholics, better than they teach anything else. These schools are a very important part of popish machinery. Every year they carry over to Rome a host of youthful and impulsive converts. Thousands of dollars are annually voted to them by unscrupulous politicians. They are going up all over the land. They are said to be free from sectarian influence. The rich and the fashionable send their children to them. But we know that they are arranged with the intent of making converts. The music, the painting, the conversation, the very atmosphere, all breathe the spirit of Romanism. Why are Romanists so anxious to educate American women? Why is it that they care so little for the women of Spain, of Mexico, of Austria? They are very anxious to educate the women of the United States; why not give a little attention to those of Rome and Italy? "Charity should begin at home." When they manifest some desire to educate the daughters of other lands, we may give them a little credit for sincerity. Until that time we shall be compelled to think that their schools and seminaries in this land are only so many ways of adding to the wealth and power of the Romish Church.

3. *They hope to gain strength by the tendency of Ritualism to the communion of Rome.*

There has been manifested of late in many churches, nominally Protestant, a painful tendency to imitate the teachings and doings of Romanism. One form after another has been introduced, until you can hardly see the difference between them and those they imitate. The whole thing is very funny; Protestants and Romanists alike despise and laugh at the curious exploits of the Ritualists. Unwilling to be called Romanists, they nevertheless have but little sympathy for their Protestant neighbors. They form a sort of connecting link in the religious world. A showman in explaining the nature of amphibious animals, said "they could not live on the land, and died in the water." So the Ritualists can not be happy in the Protestant fold, rebel against the name and its associations, yet hesitate about going over boldly to Rome.

Every now and then, some of the more advanced Ritualists go over directly to Rome. This is where they all of right belong. One of two reasons can alone deter them all from taking this step. Either they have not moral courage enough to take the step, or else, Jesuit like, they think they can do more harm to the Protestant cause, by remaining where they are. From them Rome expects much aid and comfort. They make the people familiar with her forms and ceremonies, and form a sort of connecting link, or bridge, over which thousands pass to the old "Mother Church." Ritualism would be sad enough, if it meant nothing more than ceremonies and side-shows, a sort of amusement for idiotic and superannuated clergymen. But it means more than that. It means, "We are weary of Protestant forms and doctrines, we want the ceremonies and dogmas of Popery, we want something to please the eye and delight the ear, yet something that will not set too hard upon the conscience, or require too much of the heart." May God in his mercy give the ecclesiastical body to which these men belong, the nerve and power to cast them off, so that they may be compelled to show their colors, and prevented from corrupting a church that has given to the world so many brave and true men.

4. *Romanism expects much aid from the politicians, in the subjugation of this country.* Professional politicians are men of very little principle. They are after the loaves and fishes,

seeking ever their own personal emolument. If they can gain votes by donating money to Papal institutions, by sending their daughters to Romish schools, and attending Roman Catholic churches and fairs, they will do it. This is the reason why every year hundreds of thousands of dollars are voted to Roman Catholic institutions. If Methodists, Presbyterians, or any Protestant religious body, undertake to build hospitals, or schools, or asylums, they do not ask or expect that the State will bear any part of the expense. Why is it so different with Roman Catholics? Why are they so much unlike the rest? Is it not that they hope one day to become our established church, and begin even now to anticipate their coming glory?

If a Protestant church is to be dedicated, we do not see the Governor and Mayor, Senators and Congressmen in such eager haste to attend. Politicians know that Protestants vote differently, that there is no power impelling them to think and vote in concert. They also know that the great mass of Roman Catholics vote in one way, that they act in concert; hence the eagerness with which they labor to secure their votes.

What, then, is our duty under these circumstances? We see the forces of Popery combined together for the overthrow of our civil and religious liberty. We hear the tread of their gathering hosts. Every day brings new recruits from the Old World, and furnishes them with some converts from the New. We see their churches and schools go up as by the hand of magic; while every week the Romish press grows bolder and more defiant.

1 *We must see to it, that our school system is not impaired or overthrown by them.* This is the great strength and glory of our land. Here the children of the poor, and the children of the rich meet together, drinking alike from the springs of learning. The poorest man in the land may give his children a good education. Romanism will never prevail in this land, unless she first succeeds in overthrowing our system of free public schools.

> "Fear not the skeptic's puny ire
> While near the school-house stands the spire,
> *Nor fear the bigot's iron rule,*
> While near the church spire stands the school."

We must also retain the Bible in our schools. We might as well make a stand at the first assault. Nothing will be gained by a compromise. We might as well try to compromise with the devouring flame. Let our glorious public school system stand, Bible and all, and we can bid defiance to Rome and her machinations.

2. *We must not send our children to Babylon for an education.* There are Protestant colleges and seminaries enough to select from. Shame on Protestant parents who put their children in the very gates of hell for an education. Romanism is fearfully corrupt. Her doctrines and morals, her priests and her people, are all more or less corrupt. Shall the old harlot of the seven hills educate the fair daughters of America?

3. *We must watch our politicians.* If they vote away our money to Romish institutions, we

must hold them to a strict account. A Roman Catholic cannot be trusted in office. They will surely use their influence to promote the cause of the papacy. The ballot is going to be a great power in this contest. God grant that the *ballot*, and not the *bullet*, may decide in this coming conflict.

4. *We must give no more money to support Roman Catholic institutions, to build their churches, or to pay their priests.* There is always great temptation to do this. Business men do it as a matter of policy; politicians do the same. But let our politicians and business men remember that every dollar given to Rome goes to build the prison of American hopes, drives a nail in Liberty's coffin.

5. *We must enlighten the people.* They must see and feel the impending danger. By and by it may be too late. The price of liberty is eternal vigilance. Many of our secular newspapers are under the control of Romanism. Many of our religious papers are afraid to speak out on

this subject. Some of our ministers are strangely silent. As faithful watchmen, we must give the warning. Many of the people do not know what the doctrines of the Romish Church are. They think of it as one among many other Christian churches. They forget the bloody persecutions of the past, and think that the lion has become the lamb. We must lift the veil, and show them the true nature of this Mystery of Iniquity.

6. *We must see that no one suffers in person or property, because they will not bow down to the superstitions of popery.* Religious liberty is the birthright of every American citizen. Laws must be passed by which convents shall be inspected, and those therein imprisoned restored to full liberty. The issue is before us. The conflict is upon us. It will most likely be the last great conflict between light and darkness, good and evil. Defeated here, Romanism will never bear rule over the nations of the earth again. Successful in her assaults upon this country, and she

may put the world back again into the darkness of the middle ages. But we fear no such result. God and truth must triumph. The doom of Anti-Christ is sealed. The towers of Babylon must fall.

> " Take heart! The promised hour draws near;
> I hear the downward beat of wings,
> And Freedom's trumpet sounding clear:
> Joy to the people! Woe and fear
> To new-world tyrants, old-world kings."

www.ingramcontent.com/pod-product-compliance
Lightning Source LLC
Chambersburg PA
CBHW031738230426
43669CB00007B/399